BEING HUMAN ~~~~ **~~~~~~~~~~~** ~~~~~
DELIVERING A ~~~~ **~~~~ATED RESULTS**

THE NEW
LEADERSHIP
PLAYBOOK

ANDREW BRYANT

The New Leadership Playbook: Being human whilst successfully delivering accelerated results.
© Andrew Bryant 2022

Printing: Gráfica Manuel Barbosa & Filhos, Lda.
DP: 499 957/22

ISBN: 978-1-922757-00-5 (paperback)
         978-1-922757-74-6 (eBook)

A catalogue record for this book is available from the National Library of Australia

Editors: Jason Martin, Chloe Cran, and Sarah Kate Hill
Printed in Australia by Ocean Reeve Publishing
www.oceanreevepublishing.com
Published by Andrew Bryant and Ocean Reeve Publishing

FOREWORD

"Just relax" Andrew said. This was our first meeting. Not a boardroom, but a physiotherapist's table. Some gentle neck muscle movement and then *crack*. With the neck now back in good shape, attention turned to all the other aching parts of my back.

There's nothing like a physical therapy session to allow time for a deep conversation. For Andrew I'm sure it was helpful in distracting and relaxing me. For me, it was an opportunity to learn that this man, already an expert at working with the body, was now setting his intent on becoming a master of the mind. But more than that... to become a teacher, a coach, a motivator for others.

I feel deeply fortunate to have met Andrew at this time. I was only 30, a young software entrepreneur, full of ambition and curiosity, but lacking many of the skills to be a successful leader. Our journey together started with me asking Andrew to help my sales organization develop better communication skills. I think I have generally good instincts about people, and I could see that this guy was special. Our relationship quickly evolved into executive coaching, and even further into becoming a facilitator and advisor for my company's C-Suite. A year or so after we met, I recall him saying, at the end of a coaching session, "there's something I want to ask you". I stopped him there and replied "I know what you want to ask. And the answer is no, I won't come to your wedding. The work you do for me is too valuable for me to risk that with friendship." Today, however, we count ourselves as close friends, such is the way young men mature and get wiser through the years.

A couple of decades since that fateful therapy session Andrew is still my coach. The experience has been transformative to me on so many levels. We've worked together through fast growth times, three massive economic downturns, and acquisitions of companies I've led. Andrew's work has correlated strongly with far better results, regardless of the situation, than I could ever have achieved on my own.

An intellectual, entrepreneur, coach, advisor, speaker, and author, it seems Andrew's work is never done. In late 2020 he floated with me the idea for a new book (his fourth). Andrew was already working on maturing leadership programs at Planful, a Silicon Valley software company, where I was CEO. Some of this work had weaved its way into the idea for this book, coupled with his decades-long, prolific learning of how people think, feel, behave, and actively manage all of that ("Self-leadership"). I was immediately enthused by the idea.

I enjoy a good management and leadership book. But all too often these books follow the same formula, are too conceptual, and don't have sustained impact for the readers. Andrew's approach, to write a book that was founded on science and research, but super pragmatic, resonated strongly with me. "Yes! Too many new leaders have good instincts, but they lack the pragmatic tools and skills to execute on good leadership behaviors. They need this book!" I told him.

In my experience people managers think they are leaders, but many fail to be *successful* leaders. Even the ones who've had successful results will attest that too many aspects of leadership are harder than they ought to be. For example, most leaders aren't very good at giving constructive feedback, or having a difficult conversation, or embedding values and key behaviors into the daily fabric of work life.

The New Leadership Playbook changes all that. This book gives new, and established leaders ultra-pragmatic "plays" for most of the people and culture challenges they will face in their careers. The plays are backed by reasoning and research, so you can understand the "why" behind them. When you read this book, you'll fast forward your leadership maturity by decades.

I'm not sure this will be Andrew's last book but one way or the other it will form a major part of his legacy, impacting many thousands of lives, directly and through his coaching. I've been privileged to be a recipient of his knowledge and wisdom through all these years, and I'm so glad this is now available to everyone.

Grant Halloran
CEO – Planful.com

Praise for The New Leadership Playbook

'The New Leadership Playbook weaves powerful principles and proven strategies to empower leaders to unlock potential and accelerate growth in today's increasingly accelerated, uncertain and competitive world. Written with deep insight, heart and humor, Andrew Bryant has unpacked theory into practical plays you can immediately apply to lead yourself and others to higher ground. Read, apply and reap the results. '

—Dr Margie Warrell, Senior Partner,
Korn Ferry CEO & Leadership and
Bestselling Author of Stop Playing Safe and You've Got This!

'He did it again! Once again Andrew Bryant wrote a book that is eye-opening, practical, easy to read, fun, to the point, and future oriented. I read Andrew´s book on Self-Leadership, close to 10 years ago and I can honestly say that it changed my life, made me a better leader for myself and a better leader for others. In this book, 'The New Leadership Playbook', I believe Andrew will improve many individuals´ job satisfaction and therewith their quality of life. By, in a playful way, showing leaders how to be better leaders, for themselves and for others; employees, organizations, and communities.'

—Herdis Pala Palsdottir,
Experienced Leader, Management Consultant

'Andrew Bryant's latest book, 'The New Leadership Playbook', is not only a delight to read, but also a 'right-for-the-moment' guide to what it takes to be a leader right now, as we recognize the need to build a new leadership model for a new world. I loved that it was full of stories – both the authors and other people's experiences – along with simple formulas that are well structured and easy to follow. It really is a delight to read. Do yourself a favour and grab a copy of this excellent and riveting read. It really should be on the list of must-reads for all leaders and aspiring leaders. Yes, it's that good.'

—Andrea T Edwards, author,
Uncommon Courage: an invitation.

'Andrew's talent to capture what we - business leaders - feel during difficult moments and how it influences our decisions brings a totally new dimension to management. Absolutely worth the reflection for current and future business leaders!'

—Gustavo Hildenbrand,
General Manager, Danone

'Congratulations!!! This is truly a bible/manual for leaders (with or without titles) as well as those aspiring to be leaders. The first thing that I observed about the book is a mix of balance or yin and yang which is so rare. For instance, weaving together 'being human' and 'delivering accelerated results', detailing both the leaderships 'principles' (theory) and 'plays' (practice), encompassing both 'mindset' and 'behaviors'. That makes it a practical, comprehensive, go-to-guide that is set to create a sustainable and positive change in leading being humans while creating accelerated results. It is a well-researched book that is made simple for the readers with the generous use of metaphors, cases and reflection that help imbibe the concepts easily.'

—Lakshmi Ramachandran, PhD,
Learning & Development Specialist

'Andrew Bryant is the world authority on self-leadership and the person I myself go to for guidance on the subject. When Mr Selfleadership writes a book on leadership you should not just pay attention, you should get your own copy.'

—Fredrik Haren,
The Creativity Explorer

'This is such a welcome Playbook. As managing director of Asia's #1 Executive Peer Network, I see this as an important guide for leaders in a post-covid world. We have engaged Andrew Bryant to speak at our events over the last 8-years and he always delivers impact and insights, now you can read his playbook.'

—Nick Jonsson, MD at EGN Singapore &
Indonesia, author of Executive Loneliness

'Our world is evolving at an increasingly fast pace. Organisations are facing higher levels of disruption, uncertainty, and volatility in their environments. Teams and individuals alike are having to develop greater agility, resilience, and collaboration to succeed. This 'next normal' requires a revised playbook for leaders to grow, perform and thrive.

Through his work – 'The New Leadership Playbook' – Andrew Bryant delivers an engaging, easy-to-read, and practical book for leaders, teams, and organizations to stay future-fit and play to their potential in today's world. The models, stories, and lessons which Andrew shares through 'plays and principles' are the highlights why you should read and share this book in your journey to be a human leader delivering exceptional results.'

—Manish Bundhun,
Author of 'Shots of Insights' and
'Disruptor', Chief People and
Transformation Executive, Executive Coach.

'If you are a leader looking to take your game to the next level, then 'The New Leadership Playbook' is for you! Filled with stories, examples, and strategies from Andrew Bryant's global experience as a Leadership Expert, this book is a must have for accelerated results in your career.'

—Dr Jerome Joseph,
Best Selling Author,
Global Brand Thought Leader

"The New Leadership Playbook' is a first-of-its-kind guide to managing and leading in current time. Presented in Andrew Bryant's inimitable forceful straight-talking style, it augments his time-tested self-leadership principles, that have helped many become the best version of themselves, with how to successful lead others. He has brilliantly provided mindsets and strategies, akin to sports plays that are sure to accelerate your results in the world of business.'

—Ganesh Krishnan, CIO / CTO /
Digital Transformation Leader /
VP IT at ComfortDelGro

'Given the constant crises managing anything, especially global supply chains, has never been harder. Andrew Bryant's latest book gives a much-needed solid framework for managers and leaders to sail their ship through the stormy weather!'

—Radu Palamariu,
Managing Director, Alcott Global

"The New Leadership Playbook' is packed with no-nonsense answers to real life challenges. It will feel like Andrew is coaching you on the leadership principles and 'plays' that will up your game to champions level.'

Ricardo J. Vargas,
Author of Chief Executive Team,
CEO at Consulting House

ABOUT THE AUTHOR

Andrew Bryant is the founder of Self Leadership International www.selfleadership.com and the world's leading expert on self-leadership. He has written two books on the topic: *Self Leadership: How to Become a More Successful, Efficient, and Effective Leader From the Inside Out* (Bryant & Kazan, 2012) and *Self Leadership: 12 Powerful Mindsets & Methods to Win in Life & Business* (Bryant, 2016). He has also contributed to many blogs, books, and articles on self-leadership and leadership.

Andrew has coached hundreds of leaders and leadership teams to become the best version of themselves and to scale their companies. He has international experience with clients from Asia, Australasia, the United States of America (USA), Europe, the Middle East, and Africa.

Not only has Andrew worked across geographical locations and cultures, but he has also transformed and developed leaders across industries, including the airline industry, software and hardware companies, pharmaceutical manufacturers, professional services, banking, finance, manufacturing, hospitality, and travel.

Perhaps his flexibility and agility are because, whilst he lives in Portugal, he is British by birth, Australian by passport, managing director of a Singaporean company, and Brazilian by wife!

Andrew is a highly engaging, informative, and inspiring speaker. He has spoken on stages around the world to audiences as large as 12,000, but can also connect via video conference from his fully equipped studio in Portugal.

Andrew's passion for self-leadership, seeing options, and seizing opportunities began early in his career. Qualifying as a physiotherapist in 1982, and after working in a London teaching hospital, Andrew began to work with athletes and sports teams. Curious about what makes the difference in human performance, he engaged in further studies, including acupuncture, hypnosis, neurolinguistic programming, neurosemantics, and coaching.

These disciplines formed the early framework of his self-leadership model. Whilst studying leadership at the University of Western Australia, he was struck by the need for a practical and behavioral approach to personal mastery and leadership.

After low-cost, high-volume gyms disrupted his fitness and wellness business in 2000, Andrew committed to full-time coaching, writing, and speaking. He was hired by the young CEO of a software company, Orbis Mandatum, to coach him and his executives. The CEO's review speaks to two of Andrew's values: transformation and impact. 'The results were transformational and contributed to extraordinary business results.'

A contract to teach coaching for Singapore Airlines saw Andrew relocate to Asia in 2004.

He was the President of Asia Professional Speakers Singapore (APSS) from 2015 to 2016, is a TEDx speaker, and has been on the external faculty for Singapore Management University's Women in Leadership and Executive Education programs.

View Andrew's YouTube Channel Here:

Andrew is married to Andrea, who originates from Rio do Janeiro, Brazil. He has two children from a former marriage and is now a stepdad. Whilst he enjoys the excitement of the big stage or conducting a senior leadership retreat, he is most fond of his work teaching self-esteem and self-confidence to disadvantaged and at-risk teenagers.

WHY THIS LEADERSHIP BOOK?

One of my Silicon Valley clients, Planful Inc, provided the catalyst to writing this book. Planful is a financial planning and analysis (FP&A) software company, and the chief people officer is Melissa Dreuth (Mel). Mel had experienced the effectiveness of my coaching for the executive leadership team and wanted to scale the capabilities of the company's frontline and first-time managers. In addition, she was looking for a framework for the leadership team to develop their people.

To address this need, and with input from Mel, I designed and delivered a series of online workshops and created a framework for managing people. Planful used this framework to create a manager's handbook called *The Planful Way*. I have expanded the framework and added leadership principles and stories from other clients to create this book.

In nearly twenty-five years of writing and speaking about coaching and facilitating leadership, clients often ask me, 'What is the best leadership book?' or 'If I was to read one leadership book, what would it be?'

Best is subjective and depends on where a leader is on their journey. So I thought about what would be essential to cover, what would be effective, and what could be easily applied?

These questions needed to be answered in a new context because of the challenges of living and working with and post-COVID-19. People have adjusted to working from home and, although some have returned to the office, they are doing so for only a couple of days per week. Leading such a distributed group of people, empathizing with them whilst aligning them to a culture and holding them accountable for results, needed a new playbook—a new leadership playbook.

In taking up the challenge and writing this playbook, I have focused on the problems that my clients have faced and are still facing. Thousands of coaching conversations with managers and C-level executives, and dialogues with human resources and learning and development professionals, have given me insights into the common problems leaders face and the solutions they need. I paid particular attention to the principles and practices that could be learned and applied in our current and future environment. Or, as one of the reviewers of an early draft called it, 'An MBA in a day!'

Whilst working on the book, one of my coaching clients was Amit. Amit was anxious. He was up for a significant promotion as a senior leader in a very well-known tech company. His anxiety was not unfounded; despite being an excellent individual contributor, focused, and results-driven, he had previously failed as a people manager.

'What did you learn about that experience?' I asked him.

'I wasn't clear about what I wanted from the team. I expected them to know what to do, and I wasn't very good at holding them accountable when they didn't deliver, so I did the work myself.'

This refreshing honesty made Amit very coachable. I assured him that his challenge was not unique. I had helped many managers, like him, develop their leadership and influence capital.

Not everyone has Amit's self-awareness and growth mindset. The people who are more difficult to coach and likely to plateau in their career are, surprisingly, those who have experienced too much winning. People who are promoted for achieving early results can develop a belief, resulting in a fixed mindset:

I behave this way, and I am successful—therefore, I must be successful because I behave this way.

The reality is that we are often successful because we do some things right, despite the many things we do wrong that later work against us. I have lost count of the briefings I have had from human resource professionals about a potential coachee who has climbed the corporate ladder because of results or perceived potential but is now a liability with concerns or complaints about their behavior.

Shortly after we started the coaching assignment, Amit received his promotion, and I helped him establish himself as a people leader. Together we discussed how to set the vision for the team, co-create goals, hold people accountable for performance, and have the tough conversations when they didn't.

This book is written for people like Amit and anyone who wants to understand and empathize with people whilst simultaneously driving for accelerated results.

I like to use stories, metaphors, and analogies to make a point. This book is full of stories from real managers and leaders, like Amit, facing real situations. An analogy I often use when talking about leadership is driving a car. As the driver, you have the thrill of being in control and the responsibility for yourself, your passengers, and other road users. To drive a car, you don't need to understand the intricacies of how an internal combustion engine works, but it helps to understand engine revolutions and gears to drive efficiently.

In this book, I aim not to burden you with leadership or psychological theory but to show you how to be a good driver, a driver for accelerated results.

The New Leadership Framework, Figure 1, is a guide for your success.

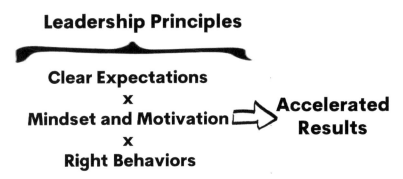

Figure 1: The Leadership Framework

This book is a handbook for you, as a manager and leader, to drive responsibly for accelerated results. Accelerated results are results that arrive quickly because you have applied leadership principles that guide you in behaving as a leader and creating the right behaviors in your people and team. When driving a car, quickly arriving at your destination is not just about pushing down hard on the accelerator; it requires being in the right gear, managing your speed around bends, and choosing the best route depending on traffic conditions. Following the leadership framework and principles in this book will influence you to set clear expectations, which will positively influence individual and team motivation, which will influence the right behaviors that drive accelerated results.

As you become familiar with the New Leadership Framework, you can use it as a quick diagnostic tool. If you are not getting results from your team or an individual, first ask yourself:

- Did I set clear expectations?
- Are people motivated to achieve?
- What behaviors were used, and are they the correct ones?

Notice that the behavior comes last because the behavior is always framed (influenced) by clear expectations and motivation. Remember that as a manager, it's easy to focus on behaviors that don't deliver results, but these behaviors might result from you not setting expectations effectively or not getting buy-in and, therefore, the right motivation.

I am not the only person thinking and writing about the future of work and leadership. Research (Mckinsey 2021) has looked at the kind of jobs that will be lost and created as automation, artificial intelligence (AI), and robotics take hold.

I spoke with Marco Dondi, one of the authors of *Defining the skills citizens will need in the future world of work* (Dondi et al., 2021) that identified fifty-six elements that will become increasingly important. These elements are a mix of competency, skills, and mindset and have been divided into four clusters or categories.

Digital fluency is not a surprise but will not be covered in this book, as we will focus on the human element of leadership. However, self-leadership, interpersonal, and cognitive skills are covered, three-fourths of what you need to future-proof yourself and your team.

So, why this leadership book? Because the practical principles and plays contained in this book have been distilled from conversations and interviews with people who wanted to get better at leading. Each play has been tested and is grounded in psychology and leadership theory and works because it's how humans work.

COGNITIVE		INTERPERSONAL	
CRITICAL THINKING -STRUCTURED PROBLEM SOLVING -LOGICAL REASONING -UNDERSTANDING BIASES -SEEKING RELEVANT INFORMATION	PLANNING AND WAYS OF WORKING -WORK PLAN DEVELOPMENT -TIME MANAGEMENT AND PRIORITIZATION -AGILE THINKING	MOBILIZING SYSTEMS -ROLE MODELING -WIN-WIN NEGOTIATIONS -CRAFTING AN INSPIRING VISION -ORGANIZATIONAL AWARENESS	DEVELOPING RELATIONSHIPS -EMPATHY -INSPIRING TRUST -HUMILITY -SOCIABILITY
COMMUNICATION -STORYTELLING AND PUBLIC SPEAKING -ASKING THE RIGHT QUESTIONS -SYNTHESIZING MESSAGES -ACTIVE LISTENING	MENTAL FLEXIBILITY -CREATIVITY AND IMAGINATION -TRANSLATING KNOWLEDGE TO DIFFERENT CONTEXTS -ADOPTING A DIFFERENT PERSPECTIVE -ADAPTABILITY -ABILITY TO LEARN	TEAMWORK EFFECTIVENESS -FOSTERING INCLUSIVENESS -MOTIVATING DIFFERENT PERSONALITIES -RESOLVING CONFLICTS -COLLABORATION -COACHING -EMPOWERING	

SELF-LEADERSHIP	DIGITAL
SELF-AWARENESS AND SELF-MANAGEMENT -UNDERSTANDING OWN EMOTIONS AND TRIGGERS -SELF-CONTROL AND REGULATION -UNDERSTANDING OWN STRENGTHS -INTEGRITY -SELF-MOTIVATION AND WELLNESS -SELF-CONFIDENCE	DIGITAL FLUENCY AND CITIZENSHIP -DIGITAL LITERACY -DIGITAL LEARNING -DIGITAL COLLABORATION -DIGITAL ETHICS
ENTREPRENEURSHIP -COURAGE AND RISK-TAKING -DRIVING CHANGE AND INNOVATION -ENERGY, PASSION, AND OPTIMISM -BREAKING ORTHODOXIES	SOFTWARE USE AND DEVELOPMENT -PROGRAM LITERACY -DATA ANALYSIS AND STATISTICS -COMPUTATION AND ALGORITHMIC THINKING
GOALS ACHIEVEMENT -OWNERSHIP AND DECISIVENESS -ACHIEVEMENT ORIENTATION -GRIT AND PERSISTENCE -COPING WITH UNCERTAINTY -SELF-DEVELOPMENT	UNDERSTANDING DIGITAL SYSTEMS -DATA LITERACY -SMART SYSTEMS -CYBERSECURITY LITERACY -TECH TRANSLATION AND ENABLEMENT

Figure 2: Future of Work Elements

Below you will see a QR code. This is your key to a gateway, behind which is extra content, including videos and downloads, worksheets, and updates to amplify and consolidate your learning. Simply point your smartphone camera at the QR code, which will take you to a login area, where you can set your password. Go there now to download your first resource.

CONTENTS

TABLE OF FIGURES

HOW TO READ AND USE THIS PLAYBOOK

I love playing chess. It's a game of tactics and strategy, and it is also a great metaphor for life. To improve at chess, you start by studying openings. Each opening has a name, such as the King's Pawn, The Queen's Gambit, and The Sicilian Game. The objective of the opening is to control the center, get the king safe, and achieve a playable middle-game position.

So, when you play chess, you have some lines (a series of moves) in mind to achieve your objective, and you are vigilant as to how all the pieces on the board are moved. Memorizing openings and lines of attack are not enough; you must understand the principles behind each move.

In sports such as American football, set moves are often called a play. The aim is to move the ball down the field, but there are various plays to achieve this. Coaches and players keep a record of these plays in a playbook.

When you lead people, you need to understand the principles of leadership and have plays for your team to effectively execute and achieve objectives. This book contains seven leadership principles to develop yourself as a leader and twelve plays to develop your team and scale your organization.

I interviewed Dirk-Peter van Leeuwen, Senior Vice President at Red Hat. I asked him if he had any advice for new leaders. He said:

> My advice is trust in yourself to play the long game. So often, I see leaders that I develop or I coach, and they are very impatient. And they're like, I need this career set now, if I don't get it, I'm moving to another company, not realizing that they may be so close to where they want to be. I would say stick with it; believe in yourself. But don't run away to the next company because you're going to have to prove yourself all over again. I see people in my organization, the most successful ones have the longest tenure, and they have stuck with it. And they've grown and grown and keep growing. And that, to me, is a very, very important lesson to learn.

This is great advice. I was self-taught at chess, and then I taught my teenage son. After a while, he started to beat me. I then started playing with one of my mastermind buddies, and he beat me. So, I realized I would need to study the principles of chess and learn some plays. Now, when I play, I experiment with new lines of attack and defense, and whether I win or lose, I am improving and can analyze the principles behind what worked and what didn't.

Reading a book on chess won't make you a grandmaster. Just as reading a book on tennis won't get you to win Wimbledon, you must study and practice. To develop your leadership, follow the principles in this book and practice the plays. Be prepared to play the long game.

There are plays in sport that have gone down in history. Plays like Diego Maradona and 'the hand of God' in the 1986 World Cup semi-finals, the 'immaculate reception' by Franco Harris in the

1972 National Football League (NFL) playoffs, or Brandi Chastain scoring on the fifth penalty kick to win the 1999 Women's World Cup. There are hundreds more, and they stand apart not due to the play itself but to the situation leading up to the play, the actions of the players in the moment, and how the play determined the outcome of the game.

The plays you learn in this book will not be as public, but they will become part of your legacy—a legacy of becoming the best version of yourself, developing your people and teams, and achieving objectives.

This book is a collection of ideas and actions that connect and influence each other in various ways. They make sense to me, but my goal is for you, the reader, to not just get a set of tools but to masterfully use these tools to create something functional and beautiful. To achieve this goal, you might read and use this book differently depending on your needs and learning style.

The book is arranged into five parts:

- Part 1: What is Leadership?
- Part 2: A Leadership Framework for Accelerated Results
- Part 3: Leadership Plays
- Part 4: Leadership Principles
- Part 5: The Future of Work

Are you more of a *why* or a *how* person?

How people will want to get their hands on the plays first and see if the tools I provide here fit their needs. If that's you, you can read Part 3 before Part 4.

Why people are more likely to want to understand the big picture and see the leadership principles. If that's you, you can read Part 4 before Part 3.

Regardless of your style, I recommend you first read Part 1: What is Leadership? and Part 2: A Leadership Framework for Accelerated Results, as these set up the premise for the plays and the principles.

It is sometimes said that management is doing things right, but leadership is doing the right things. In other words, management is transactional, and leadership is transformational. However, in the reality of day-to-day business, we are both managing and leading. Therefore, I will use the terms management and leadership interchangeably throughout this book.

I hope this book becomes a companion in your leadership journey, and you will refer to it many times. If you are a leader of managers, you may wish to provide this book for your managers, and if you are looking for a customized solution for your company, I can be reached at www.selfleadership.com or on LinkedIn www.linkedin.com/in/andrewbryant/.

PART 1: WHAT IS LEADERSHIP?

There are almost as many definitions of leadership as the number of people who have attempted to define the concept.

—B M Bass

Before we explore the principles that will drive your behaviors to be a successful leader, I think it's worth taking a moment to consider what leadership is, what counts as success, and whether there is anything NEW.

I often get asked who my favorite leader is, and my answer is always, 'It depends.' Leadership is always about context.

Genghis Khan (1158–1227 CE) united the nomadic tribes of Northeast Asia and created the Mongol Empire, which became the largest contiguous empire in history after his death. But historians describe his conquests as destruction on an unprecedented scale resulting in mass exterminations and famine. He was a successful leader, but would you have wanted to work for him?

Steve Jobs led Apple to massive success, but his management style was autocratic. He was notorious for his high expectations, impatience, and relentless passion for his company.

> In the Macintosh Division, you had to prove yourself every day, or Jobs got rid of you. He demanded excellence and kept you at the top of your game. It wasn't easy to work for him; it was sometimes unpleasant and always scary, but it drove many of us to do the finest work of our careers. (Kawasaki, 2019)

The leadership definition that I find most practical is: 'Leadership is the process of influencing others in a manner that enhances their contribution to the realization of group goals.' (Platow et al., 2019)

With this definition, the measure of your success as a leader is not whether you unite tribes like Genghis Kahn or are a brilliant entrepreneur like Steve Jobs, but whether you influence people to enhance their contribution. Now you can see why I selected this definition, because it's about being human and delivering accelerated results.

I believe that the challenge for leadership in the 'new normal' environment is having respect and empathy for people while holding them accountable to realize their individual and group goals.

A growing number of chief executive officers (CEOs), including Jack Welch (GE), Jack Ma (Alibaba), Paul Polman (ex-Unilever), and most recently Marc Benioff (Salesforce), are going on record as saying that maximizing shareholder value is idiotic. We must move to maximize stakeholder value.

Benioff wrote in his 2004 book *Compassionate Capitalism*:

> The competitive advantage you gain from being a caring and sharing company is significant; it instills in your people a higher integrity level. In turn, stakeholders want to be associated with a company that has heart.

So, what's new for leadership is a focus on stakeholder value, as said by the CEOs above, and compassion. Or is that new?

Legendary Indian Emperor Ashoka (Aśoka 304–233 BCE) ruled humanely after his conversion to Buddhism. He issued edicts carved on stone pillars in the local language of each region that exhorted citizens to generosity, piety, justice, and mercy. Ashoka also adopted and promoted a policy of respect and tolerance for people of all faiths.

So, caring leadership is not new, and perhaps there is a cyclical nature to such things. But with the acceleration of digitization and automation, I hope leaders will focus on bringing out what is uniquely human. Research backs up my hope. Refer to the fifty-six elements identified by McKinsey that I shared in my opening: Why this Leadership Book?

Leadership principles frame a leader's behavior. Values also influence the leader's behavior, so the terms values and principles could be used interchangeably, but to my mind, a principle is more concrete and gives a clearer indication of the required behavior.

My friend, Dr Fons Trompenaars, author of *Riding the Waves of Culture* (Trompenaars & Hamden-Turner, 1996), describes the value of a value as its ability to reconcile a dilemma. I was interviewing Fons in 2019, and he shared with me the case of CDPQ, a large institutional investor that manages pension plans and insurance programs in Quebec, Canada. The company's values were ambition, innovation, and collaboration, but during the 2008 global financial crisis, these values saw them lose nearly ten percent of their worth and nearly destroyed the company.

When they analyzed what happened, they realized, 'We were very ambitious, so we took too many risks. We were innovative, so we did it with innovative products, and because of collaboration, we couldn't name anybody to be accountable'.

Dr Trompenaars gave them some input, and they came up with:

- Ambition through Prudence
- Innovation through Discipline
- Collaboration through Individual Accountability.

Now they had six values, of which three are opposites. The company's leaders asked themselves, *What does it mean to be ambitious with prudence?' 'What does it mean to collaborate with individual accountability?* Since then, the recovery and growth of CDPQ have been a testament to this approach.

Some years ago, I had a similar experience with Vopak, a Dutch independent multinational company that stores and handles products ranging from chemicals, oil, gases, and liquified natural gas (LNG) to biofuels and vegetable oils. They asked me to run a workshop to help them translate their values into behaviors in a Southeast Asian context. The value that stood out for me was 'disciplined entrepreneurship'.

This is also a good example of how paired-opposite values can become guiding principles for behaviors. Entrepreneurship without discipline behaves like a start-up, and discipline without entrepreneurship leads to stagnation.

Dr Trompenaars calls this the sandbox paradigm. As a parent, you say to your children: 'Listen, children, you can play inside the sandbox, but don't go outside of it.' This approach increases their freedom within the center. It creates a safe space to play.

Leadership books and memes on the internet often talk about leadership as if there's one right way to do it. 'Telling is bad, listening is good', or 'Focusing on profits is bad, focusing on compassion and community is good'. Such blanket statements about what constitutes good leadership ignore context.

Imagine you are on an airplane flying at 41,000 feet. You are watching an inflight movie when *bang*, there's a loud noise, and the oxygen masks fall from overhead. Would you prefer the captain says over the intercom:

a) 'Ladies and gentlemen, we have a problem, and I really value your feelings and ideas. What I'd like you to do is form focus groups of five to seven people and come up with ways I could handle this problem.'

or

b) 'Ladies and gentlemen, we have a problem. I need you all to sit down and fasten your seat belts whilst I fly us out of it. It might be a bit uncomfortable for a short while, but I will get you to the ground safely.'

You chose b), right?

Successful leadership style is dependent on context and the motivation and capability of the people to contribute to the solution. Your opinion is not useful unless you have experience flying that kind of plane.

Path–Goal Theory (House, 1971), provides a model of the interaction between leadership style, environmental factors, and employee motivation.

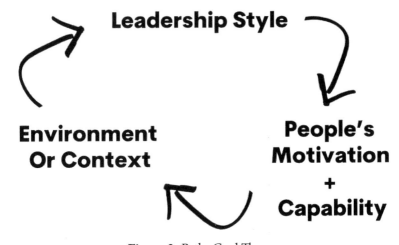

Figure 3: Path–Goal Theory

Path–Goal Theory suggests a leader follows these three basic steps:

1. Determine the employee and environmental characteristics
2. Select a leadership style
3. Focus on motivational factors that will help the employee succeed.

We will look at points 1 and 2 later in this book, but for now, let's focus on leadership style.

House & Mitchell (1974) defined four types of leadership behaviors or styles based on two factors: relationship (empathy) and task orientation (accountability). They are:

1. **Directive**: The directive leader is task-oriented and typically tells followers what is expected of them, how to perform a task, and schedules and coordinates work. It is most effective when people are unsure about the task or when there is low structure or ambiguity within the environment.

2. **Supportive**: The Supportive Leader is relationship-oriented and aims to make work pleasant for the workers by showing concern for them and being friendly and approachable. It is most effective when tasks and relationships are physically or psychologically challenging.

3. **Participative**: The Participative Leader is also relationship-oriented and tends to consult with employees before making decisions. This style is most effective when subordinates are competent with high autonomy (control).

4. **Achievement**: The Achievement Leader sets challenging goals (task-oriented), expects workers to perform at their highest level, and shows confidence in their ability to meet this expectation (relationship-oriented). This style is most effective in professional work environments (technical or scientific) or achievement environments (sales).

As a leader, you will have a default and a secondary leadership style, but since people and situations change, so must you adapt. There is some debate amongst leadership academics as to whether this is possible. Some say pick the leader for the situation (contingency theory) whilst others believe the leader can adjust their style (path–goal theory).

Without naming names, I know a leader who has the human touch, is a great listener and participative motivator, but when things got tough, even though she tried to be more directive, she failed to make the shift and was fired as CEO. I also know a very directive leader whose drive established his start-up as ready for acquisition, but when he received feedback in the early stages of the pandemic about being more human, his message was, 'I hope you and your family are OK, but don't miss a target.'

Not every manager wants to grow or sees leadership as a skill that needs to be constantly honed. One of this book's leadership principles is that leaders are learners, so it is written for people who have the courage and passion to be the best version of themselves.

People don't leave good companies; they leave bad managers. This maxim has been quoted so often by so many people that it is taken as gospel, but there's no conclusive evidence to back this assertion. Culture Amp, an online engagement platform, reports combining available information with the data from 175 teams (greater than eight people) of the world's fastest-growing companies. They were looking for what was driving employee retention at any given company. They discovered:

1. People leave bad managers, but it is not the number one reason people leave a company.
2. In 'good' companies, managers make a difference.
3. In 'bad' companies, good or bad managers make little to no difference to a person's decision to leave.

In my experience as a coach and leadership consultant, I am not surprised by these findings. If the culture of a company is toxic, or its systems are not human-centric, these plays will be as useful as lipstick on a pig.

Mariam is a senior vice president of product management. She came to me for coaching to develop her leadership skills. Whilst we made progress on her ability to manage herself and delegate effectively, her insight and ideas were falling on deaf ears at her previous company. Finally, she left and joined a new organization. I caught up with her recently, and she said, 'I'm in a completely different situation (a good one) from where I was before. It made me realize that there is a dimension in leadership about one's fit with the organization and how much that can play a role in career development and progression.'

So, assuming you are working for an organization that values leadership, what makes a good manager and what makes a bad one? It simply comes down to behaviors.

I do not yet know of a man who became a leader as a result of having undergone a leadership course.

—Singapore's first prime minister,
Lee Kuan Yew (LKY)

So much for MBAs! And should I be out of a job? But wait, LKY had a point. Leadership frameworks are useful, but unless we practice and adjust our leadership behaviors in the real and changing world—we will likely be unsuccessful.

One mindset will undermine everything I am sharing in this book, and that is the belief that great leaders are born, not made.

Consider some great leaders: Churchill, John F Kennedy (JFK), Gandhi, Mandela. These leaders have character traits such as initiative, courage, intelligence, and humor, which are likely to be innate, and so, therefore, leaders are born, not made! Or so the argument goes.

The problem is that this argument works backwards and assumes causation. It ignores situations and environments that stimulate individuals to develop leadership. This argument also perpetuates the bias that leadership traits are those closely associated with being male. Attributes such as empathy, understanding, and collaboration are largely ignored.

In the future, there will be no female leaders. There will just be leaders.

—Sherryl Sandberg

In addition, traits can only be inferred through behaviors, says my friend and colleague, Dr Paul Englert, an expert on psychometrics. Since behaviors are mostly learned, leaders are most definitely developed. So keep reading, keep learning, and keep developing!

Much research has been done on leadership behaviors, including a progressive program at Google named Project Oxygen. This research identified a strong relationship between ten behaviors (Figure 4) and managers being rated as effective by their employees.

DN Prasad, a former 'Googler' (Director, Google People Services, APAC), shared his experiences with Project Oxygen. 'I was not part of the research that came out of Mountainview, California, but when the results came out in 2008, I was involved in the rollout.'

DN Prasad had led teams at his previous company. He joined Google in India and then moved to Singapore as the chief of staff for the head of human resources for the region. I, therefore, inquired if the management behaviors need to be customized for the country or culture.

'It starts with the hiring. Google hires people who can perform their roles and move across regions, so there was no customization. Instead of one company, you would have ten companies in ten countries. We always aimed to have a balance between respect for the local culture and what makes a Googler everywhere.'

Google's rollout of Project Oxygen used a Four E approach: education, exposure, experience, and engagement. Once all the managers had attended workshops on the ten behaviors and a new manager onboarding process was in place, the company instituted upwards feedback, so managers would find out how they were doing.

From 2016, this feedback against the framework became part of the performance review process. Of course, it was important

REFLECTION:
LOOK AT THE LIST OF BEHAVIORS BELOW AND GIVE YOURSELF A RATING FROM 1 (LOW) TO 7 (HIGH) ON HOW YOU RATE EACH OF YOUR BEHAVIORS.

	YOUR CURRENT RATING						
IS A GOOD COACH	1	2	3	4	5	6	7
EMPOWERS THE TEAM AND DOES NOT MICROMANAGE	1	2	3	4	5	6	7
CREATES AN INCLUSIVE TEAM ENVIRONMENT, SHOWING CONCERN FOR SUCCESS AND WELL-BEING	1	2	3	4	5	6	7
IS PRODUCTIVE AND RESULTS-ORIENTED	1	2	3	4	5	6	7
IS A GOOD COMMUNICATOR WHO LISTENS AND SHARES INFORMATION	1	2	3	4	5	6	7
SUPPORTS CAREER DEVELOPMENT AND DISCUSSES PERFORMANCE	1	2	3	4	5	6	7
HAS A CLEAR VISION/ STRATEGY FOR THE TEAM	1	2	3	4	5	6	7
HAS KEY TECHNICAL SKILLS TO HELP ADVISE THE TEAM	1	2	3	4	5	6	7
COLLABORATES ACROSS THE ORGANIZATION	1	2	3	4	5	6	7
IS A STRONG DECISION MAKER	1	2	3	4	5	6	7

Figure 4: Google Management Behaviors

to deliver on Objectives and Key Results (OKRs), but how you managed to achieve these results mattered, too.

Not all organizations realize the importance of balancing the how and the what—the humanity with the results. Unfortunately, they often learn too late that when good people leave such companies, they leave behind survivors swimming in a toxic culture.

Google is a developmental culture informed by a growth mindset, so when someone scores low on a particular behavior, there is training or support to address this weakness.

DN Prasad was kind enough to share his story of falling short in the first year he received the feedback:

> When at Infosys, and for my first two and half years at Google, I got a lot of accolades for my leadership and management; people from the USA, United Kingdom (UK), and India wanted to work on my team. I then had a period as an individual contributor, and then I was asked to set up a new function and had people from Ireland, Singapore, China, and Japan. It was a new function, so I needed to be very hands-on. When the feedback came in, I scored low on *Empowers team and does not micromanage.*

DN's behavior is common for people moving from individual contributor to manager. They think they must do it all themselves. The feedback gave him the awareness he needed, and for the next six months, he worked on his style, making sure people knew why they were being asked to do certain things and listening to their input.

The next time he received feedback, it was excellent, proving that leaders are learners and can improve with a framework and plays.

When you read the plays in this book, you will notice that the skills identified by Google are all addressed, except for number eight (technical skills). As a manager, you will need key technical skills to advise your team, but as a leader, you will have people reporting to you who are far more knowledgeable than you in their domain. I cover how to handle this with the leadership principle of executive presence.

The advantage of defining leadership by behaviors is they can be observed and measured in the workplace or an assessment or development center. When leaders develop and demonstrate these behaviors, they create a culture where staff can develop themselves to perform. All of which leads us to this idea:

> The purpose of leadership is not to create more followers
> but to create more leaders.

Part 2: A Framework for Accelerated Results

Leadership is not a popularity contest; it's about leaving your ego at the door. The name of the game is to lead without a title.

—Robin S Sharma

As per the leadership definition I shared earlier in this book, you must influence people towards group goals. The key word here is influence, and the simplest definition of influence is to get a willing yes. You can use force to get people to say 'yes', but to my mind, that is manipulation, or you can beg or bribe them, but that, to my mind, is persuasion.

I previously mentioned driving as a metaphor for leadership. If you have driven a manual transmission (stick shift), you will know the feeling of using the clutch and smoothly shifting gears. You will probably also know what it feels like to force the gears and have the car fight back.

Slow is smooth, smooth is fast.

—US Navy Seals

This mantra, from a group that does some of the most dangerous things in the world, is a great reminder to slow down and do the job right.

As a leader, you will need to deliver results, but by doing things smoothly and engaging your people, you can deliver accelerated results.

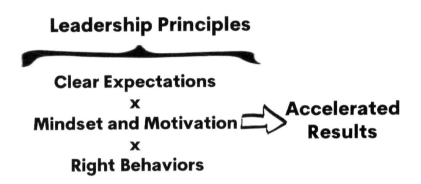

When I discussed why you should read this book, I introduced the New Leadership Framework.

Clear expectations positively influence mindset and motivation, which in turn influences the right behaviors that drive accelerated results.

This framing creates a multiplying effect and, when properly executed, will enable you to scale your results, your team, and your entire company.

Conversely, if you don't set clear expectations, if people don't have the right mindset, and if their behaviors don't align with the company's principles, you and your team will miss objectives (crash and burn).

CLEAR EXPECTATIONS

We choose to go to the moon in this decade and do the other things, not because they are easy, but because they are hard, because that goal will serve to organize and measure the best of our energies and skills, because that challenge is one that we are willing to accept, one we are unwilling to postpone, and one which we intend to win, and the others, too.

—US President John F Kennedy

In September 1962, Kennedy delivered his famous 'We choose to go to the moon' speech in front of a crowd of 40,000. The previous year, the cosmonaut Yuri Gagarin had successfully orbited the Earth, and Americans were fearful of Soviet space dominance.

The speech was remarkable, not just for its vivid pictures and soaring metaphors, but because NASA was months away from putting an astronaut in space and had no idea how it would achieve the goal. Kennedy set big and clear expectations that mobilized mindsets and behaviors that eventually led to American astronaut Neil Armstrong walking on the moon on 20 July 1969.

As a manager and leader, are you setting big and clear expectations?

First you tell people clearly what results you are looking for. Then you discuss how to get those results. (Bossidy, 2002)

Have you ever delegated a request or piece of work to someone and then said, 'Do you understand?' I'm sure you have, and they typically reply, 'Yes.' But did they understand? Possibly not. So why does this happen?

Misunderstanding happens because your expectation is in your head, and when they listen to you, they try to fit what they hear into their existing expectation. They say 'yes' because they understand *their* view of the outcome, not necessarily *yours*.

> **REFLECTION:**
> **REMEMBER A PIECE OF DELEGATED WORK WHERE THE OUTCOME DID NOT MEET YOUR EXPECTATIONS. HOW COULD YOU HAVE FRAMED YOUR REQUEST BETTER?**

Surprisingly, setting clear expectations is less about telling and more about asking. To properly set expectations, use questions like:

- What is important about this?
- How should we go about solving this?
- What is the right thing to do?

When you ask questions, you understand how a person has framed their future actions. But, if you must explain in more detail, make sure you ask them to specifically recount what they understand about the task rather than if they simply understand.

You could set the expectation for an employee to purchase a sofa, but is that a clear expectation?

Clearly not, because sofas come in different sizes, colors, materials, and prices. You could specify each of these criteria in your request, or you could be clear about where and how you want to use the sofa—for example, in the client waiting area—and ask your employee if they are comfortable making the selection based on the result you are looking for.

MINDSET + MOTIVATION

I graduated as a physiotherapist in 1982. Physiotherapy wasn't my first choice; I wanted to become a doctor but did not apply myself during my final year of school and didn't get the required grades.

Learning a valuable lesson about focus, I was determined to advance my career by working at a prestigious London teaching hospital. My mindset and motivation delivered the goal, and I started my career at University College Hospital, London.

I quickly realized that whilst assisting people to recover from injury and disease was rewarding. I was more curious about what makes humans perform optimally.

> Health is a state of complete physical, mental, and social well-being and not merely the absence of disease or infirmity. (World Health Organization, n.d.)

My curiosity started me on a journey of further studies, including acupuncture, hypnosis, philosophy, psychology, neuro-linguistic programming (NLP), and neurosemantics.

I left the hospital to work with athletes and sports teams to prepare them to win, as much as help them recover. Mindset and motivation were clearly the X factors that made the difference in both speed of recovery and winning.

A mindset is a series of self-perceptions or beliefs people hold about themselves. These determine behavior, outlook, and mental attitude. Motivation is derived from the Latin word *movere*, meaning to move. Motivation is collectively the forces acting on or within a person that cause the arousal, direction, and persistence of goal-directed, voluntary effort.

Fast forward eighteen years from my graduation, I had started my coaching and speaking business and was formulating a self-leadership methodology when a fortunate event occurred. Money was tight as a fledging consultant, so I worked part-time as a physiotherapist in a colleague's practice in North Sydney to supplement my income.

One day, I was working on a patient with a stiff neck. We chatted whilst I stretched and manipulated him back into shape. He was a young CEO trying to motivate his team to believe. I shared some ideas, and he was surprised. 'You don't talk like a physiotherapist,' he said.

I shared my story of establishing myself as an executive coach, and he said, 'Come and see me at my office. I think I need a coach.' The rest, as they say, is history.

Grant Halloran was my first CEO client, and I helped him scale himself and his start-up team to acquisition. Grant is now the CEO of Planful Inc, and we still work together, which is how I met Mel Dreuth, whose request for a first-time manager's training motivated the design of the New Leadership Framework and the writing of this book.

According to Carol S Dweck, PhD, in her book *Mindset: The New Psychology of Success* (Dweck, 2007), there are two mindsets: fixed and growth.

Having a fixed mindset creates an urgency to prove yourself—criticism is seen as an attack on your character and to be avoided. Having a growth mindset encourages learning and effort. If you truly believe you can improve at something, you will be more motivated to learn and practice. Criticism is seen as valuable feedback and openly embraced. The hallmark of the growth mindset is the passion for sticking with it, especially when things are not going well.

This playbook aligns with the growth mindset, but many managers treat their staff as if they cannot grow. This mindset leads to many of the behaviors that departing employees share in their exit interviews.

Some years ago, I was asked to coach a lawyer through the process of becoming an equity partner in a prestigious international law firm. Human Resources briefed me. 'He is an excellent lawyer. But he speaks about his associates as 'units of production' and has no patience to develop them.'

Look at Figure 5—Mindsets for People Management and see what best describes this lawyer's style.

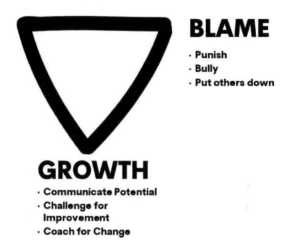

RESCUE
- Help and support others constantly
- Deny own needs
- Solve problems for others

BLAME
- Punish
- Bully
- Put others down

GROWTH
- Communicate Potential
- Challenge for Improvement
- Coach for Change

Figure 5: Mindsets for People Management

Unfortunately, perceiving his associates as units of production, he would blame them for non-performance and spend no time developing them or reflecting on how his own expectation setting was responsible for their shortcomings. Such a mindset can drive people to leave the organization or detrimentally impact the self-esteem and confidence of people who stay.

Equally non-productive is the manager who takes the role of rescuer. Rescuers are over-responsible, and with a positive intent to be nice, they inhibit the growth of their people, leading to frustration. Rescuers cannot scale their team and typically burn themselves out and plateau in their careers.

The correct mindset to adopt for yourself, and to encourage in your people, is one of growth. This mindset comes from a belief in your team's potential to learn, grow, improve, and succeed regardless of the challenges or failures ahead.

REFLECTION:

WHAT'S YOUR DEFAULT POSITION: BLAMER, RESCUER, GROWTH, OR A COMBINATION?
WHY DOES A GROWTH ATTITUDE WORK?

The Rosenthal, or Pygmalion, effect refers to the result of a study that showed if teachers expected enhanced performance from their students, then the students' performance was enhanced. The study supported the hypothesis that reality can be positively or negatively influenced by the expectations of others. So, if you expect greatness from your team, their performance will be improved.

If you think you can, or you think you can't, you're right.

—Henry Ford

REFLECTION:

USE THE LEARNING DIARY FROM THE ONLINE GATEWAY (QR CODE BELOW) TO WRITE THE NAMES OF THE PEOPLE WHO REPORT DIRECTLY TO YOU. ALONGSIDE EACH NAME, WRITE YOUR ATTITUDE ABOUT THIS PERSON. THEN ASK YOURSELF, 'IS MY MINDSET AFFECTING THEIR BEHAVIOR IN A POSITIVE OR NEGATIVE WAY?'

From a self-leadership perspective (Bryant & Kazan, 2012), you are responsible for your mindset, regardless of the circumstances. The people in your team should also be responsible for their mindset, providing you have set expectations they can buy into. But what happens when a member of your team does not have the right mindset? Can you motivate them without becoming a rescuer?

The answer lies in a formula developed by Victor Vroom PhD, a professor at Yale School of Management. (Vroom, 1964)

Motivation = Expectancy x Instrumentality x Valence

Figure 6: Expectancy Theory

Vroom's formula, known as Expectancy Theory, says that if the future seems reasonably attractive, we know how to get there, and we believe we will be appropriately rewarded, then we will be motivated to act. In other words, if people expect a positive and desirable outcome, they will usually work hard to perform at the level expected of them.

Expectancy refers to the strength of a person's belief about whether or not a specific job performance is attainable. In other words, 'If I put in the effort, will I get the results?'

The strength of this belief or self-efficacy depends on whether a person has a fixed or growth mindset and external social proof. For example, the inner dialogue could be, 'I am confident I can complete these actions' or 'I can see other people putting in effort and getting results, so I can too.'

Several factors contribute to expectancy perceptions: the level of difficulty of the task, the amount of support that may be expected from superiors and subordinates, the quality of the materials and equipment, and the availability of pertinent information.

The manager can, therefore, positively influence expectancy when setting expectations by articulating:

- This is something you are competent to do.
- Here are some examples of people who are already doing it or have done it before.
- You will have access to all the resources you need.

Instrumentality answers the question, 'If I complete certain actions, will I get the reward?'

Brains are goal-seeking machines, and when we achieve a goal, we are rewarded with the brain chemical dopamine, which makes us feel good. This good feeling tells us that this is something important and worth repeating.

As a manager, you can enhance motivation by articulating how good a person will feel when they complete the task. If you want this behavior repeated, remember to make the people feel good when the task is completed. Praise, acknowledgment, a thank you cost nothing but are highly motivating.

Valence means there must not just be a reward for effort, but the right sort of reward—and one size does not fit all.

This is where your emotions come in. Expectancy was logical, but valance is about how you will feel when you achieve the result—will you value the reward?

As a manager or leader, you must discover what's important to your people. Is it extrinsic (money, promotion, free time, benefits) or intrinsic (satisfaction, sense of achievement)? It is essential to get buy-in from your people about the importance of the task.

As you read and practice the plays from this book, remember the importance of mindset and motivation to human performance. It is also worth noting factors that will demotivate your people, include:

- no clear career progression
- unsuitable or unsafe work environment
- lack of leadership
- conflict.

Expectation and mindset work together to frame behaviors, and at the end of this section, I have provided a checklist to ensure you maximize your influence and impact.

RIGHT BEHAVIORS

Our names are labels, plainly printed on the bottled essence of our past behavior.

—Logan Pearsall Smith

If someone said they were your friend but stole your wallet and your car, would you believe what they said or did?

If you say you value health and fitness, read and talk about health and fitness, but drink, smoke, and sit on the couch eating chips, what will impact your outcomes—your values or your behaviors?

To paraphrase Newton's first law: behaviors are the force that moves a stationary body or influences its direction or velocity. In short, everything stays the same unless some behavior occurs.

You can hire for talent and skills, maybe even mindset, but you will promote or fire people for their behaviors. Yet most people struggle to articulate behaviors.

In the biographical drama film *The Pursuit of Happyness* (Muccino, 2006), we witness behaviors to gain employment at a brokerage firm. Chris Gardner, played by Will Smith, works off a call sheet to find clients and discovers that he gains an extra eight minutes per day if he doesn't hang up the phone. He also chooses to start from the top of his call sheet, connecting with the higher value prospect rather than work up from the bottom. The movie is mostly about Chris's mindset in dealing with adversity whilst caring for his son, but his behaviors get him the results. Spoiler alert: Chris Gardner did become a stockbroker and eventually founded his own brokerage firm, Gardner Rich & Co, in 1987.

If mindset and motivation are the inner game, behaviors are the outer game. Behaviors are talents, experiences, and skills put into action. Whilst mindset can be surmised, behaviors are observable and measurable. The success of a leader is measured by how their people behave or act to achieve the desired results.

Consider the following description:

Simon is a corporate manager and very ambitious. He is keen to show his work in a good light. He never hesitates to highlight his contribution to a project, but you never hear him give credit to others or admit any mistakes. You notice that he watches which way the wind is blowing before he offers an opinion.

Write down the behaviors that are described (you can use the downloadable learning diary for this).

Now look at this picture:

Figure 7: Observing Behavior

> **WHAT DO YOU OBSERVE IS HAPPENING? PLEASE WRITE DOWN YOUR OBSERVATIONS BEFORE PROCEEDING.**

Does your description contain observations, or did you make some assumptions?

Assumptions include what is happening, the roles the man and woman hold, what the man and woman are thinking and feeling. You can't know their roles and feelings because this is just an image. Some examples of assumptions that I have heard from my management students include:

- The man is the manager, and he is shouting at a subordinate who doesn't like being shouted at.
- The man is singing badly to the woman, who is covering her ears because it's so bad.
- The woman is the manager, and the man is complaining, blaming, and not taking ownership.

To observe and articulate behavior, you need to train yourself to ask specific questions:

- Who specifically is in the picture?
- What specifically are the people doing?
- When/where specifically is this happening?
- How specifically are the actions being done?
- Against what criteria are you evaluating?

Now back to Simon, the corporate manager. What specifically let you know that Simon is ambitious? What behaviors did he demonstrate that caused you to evaluate him as ambitious? Was it something he said, something he did, or was it your assumption (a mind-read)?

The specific behaviors that were absent included giving credit to others and admitting mistakes.

If you were managing or coaching Simon, you would need to set the expectation that the mindset for growth as a leader includes the behaviors of giving credit and articulating learning from your own mistakes.

As for waiting to see which way the wind blows before offering an opinion, this behavior contradicts the leadership principle of Disagree and Commit, which we will discuss later. If Simon is motivated to progress, you could help him realize that he will gain greater acknowledgment and progression if he adopts this principle.

REFLECTION:

HAVE YOU BEEN CAUGHT OUT BY MAKING THE WRONG ASSUMPTION BEFORE?

WHAT WILL YOU DO TO CHECK YOUR ASSUMPTIONS MOVING FORWARD?

In 2020, at the start of the COVID-19 pandemic, a CEO that I was coaching was struggling to lead. He felt the pressure of delivering on his promises to the board whilst facing lockdown and business disruption. I acknowledged his situation but asked him how he thought his people were feeling. This shifted his focus as he realized he wasn't the only one this situation was affecting.

'What do your people need from you?' I asked him.

'I need to show them I understand and care.' He rightly observed.

'OK, what behaviors can you engage in that will show this?'

Together we brainstormed some concrete actions that started with calling his key employees and letting them know he was there to support them, and the company would survive. His people appreciated his behavior, and the company is not just surviving but thriving despite the global disruption of COVID-19.

You will develop your ability to observe behaviors with additional plays later in this book, as we explore Feedback, Collaboration, and Decisiveness. These plays will help you improve your ability to observe and articulate behavior whilst also becoming aware of your assumptions.

For a senior leadership position, organizations will often put candidates through an assessment center. This consists of a standardized evaluation of behavior based on multiple evaluations, including job-related simulations, interviews, and/or psychological tests. Job simulations are used to evaluate candidates on behaviors relevant to the job's most critical aspects (or competencies).

Assessors are trained to make behavioral observations and avoid assumptions, which I have introduced you to in this section. Since behaviors deliver results, and you will be measured on the results you create, I encourage you to constantly improve your ability to articulate the behaviors you are looking for and acknowledge the right ones you observe from your people.

To assist you in this endeavor, here are some assumptions (biases) to be aware of and correct for:

Similar-to-me	As this person is like me, or I like them, I will judge their behaviors favorably.
Halo bias	As this person is good at one thing, I will evaluate all their behaviors as good.
Horns bias	When this person performs badly at a task, I will judge all their behaviors as below standard.
Attribution bias	Attributing task failure or success to employee mindset or behaviors when the result was due to external factors outside of their control.
Recency bias	The tendency to only comment on the most recent behavior rather than consider a history of actions.
Stereotyping	Generalizing behavior to a group of people, rather than observing the specific behavior of an individual in context.

Ideally, you will be able to observe the behaviors of the people who report to you, but in a virtual world, you may need to ask them to report on their actions and behaviors.

Here are some examples of questions you could ask to elicit this information in an interview or video call:

BEHAVIOR	QUESTION
BUILDING RELATIONSHIPS	COULD YOU PLEASE SHARE SOME EXAMPLES WHERE YOU HAVE RESOLVED CHALLENGING ISSUES WITH COLLEAGUES AND ENHANCED THE WORKING RELATIONSHIP?

COMMUNICATION	COULD YOU GIVE ME SOME EXAMPLES OF WHERE YOU HAVE COMMUNICATED A DIFFICULT MESSAGE OR PITCHED A MESSAGE TO IMPACT A PARTICULAR AUDIENCE?
VALUING DIVERSITY	HAVE THERE BEEN TIMES WHEN YOU HAVE SOUGHT INPUT OR OPINIONS FROM OTHERS, EVEN THOSE LESS SENIOR THAN YOU? PLEASE TELL ME ABOUT THEM.
DEVELOPING SELF	WHAT DO YOU CONSIDER TO BE YOUR STRENGTHS? NOW, WHAT DO YOU CONSIDER TO BE YOUR WEAKNESSES? TELL ME WHAT YOU ARE DOING TO DEVELOP YOUR STRENGTHS AND OVERCOME YOUR WEAKNESSES.
MOTIVATING OTHERS TO ACHIEVE HIGH PERFORMANCE	DO YOU CONSIDER YOURSELF TO BE A GOOD MOTIVATOR? PLEASE TELL ME ABOUT A SITUATION IN WHICH YOU HAVE ENCOURAGED OTHERS TO IMPROVE PERFORMANCE. HOW DID YOU GO ABOUT IT?
ARTICULATING VISION AND DIRECTION	WHAT IS YOUR VISION FOR YOUR TEAM'S PERFORMANCE? HAVE YOU COMMUNICATED THIS VISION, AND HOW? DO YOU HAVE BUY-IN FOR THIS VISION? HOW DO YOU KNOW?

A LEADERSHIP OPERATING SYSTEM

Everything must be made as simple as possible. But not simpler.

—Albert Einstein

Right Expectations x Mindset and Motivation x Right Behaviors provide the code for a Leadership Operating System. Whether you are a CEO leading your executive leadership team or a marketing manager running a team of young creative individuals, you can put an operating system in place for clear communication and activity.

Once upon a time, early 2007 to be exact, Nokia dominated 49.4 percent of the smartphone market. Their Symbian operating system was easy to use, and when you bought a new Nokia phone, you were up and running in no time. But in January 2007, Steve Jobs walked onto a stage, pulled out an iPhone, and changed the world forever.

Unfortunately, many managers and leaders still operate and communicate in a pre-iPhone, even analog, fashion. Jobs showcased a new operating system that drove an intuitive interface that even a child could use. Shouldn't our leadership operating system be equally effective?

The foundation of the analog operating system was, and remains, the meeting. Meetings where everybody had to show up, but nobody really knew what the meeting was about. Huge amounts of time have been wasted in meetings without clear expectations when participants aren't prepared, and the highest-paid officer (HIPO) does all the talking.

Now, we have the luxury to communicate synchronously, asynchronously, in person, virtually, by message, or by voice. Choice can lead to confusion, and as a leader, you need to set expectations about how information flows, through which channels, and when.

The BADI acronym is a useful tool to think about setting up comms.

B is for bonding. Bonding or connecting builds trust, and whilst time-consuming, it can accelerate other processes.

Depending on your personality, it can be pleasurable or an energy drain. Bonding is best done in person; however, checking in with what's happening with people and how they are feeling can be the start of any communication. For decades, bonding over drinks or golf has been a default operating system, but this is not an inclusive activity. If you want to benefit from the power of diversity, you should consider other activities to get to know people and for them to get to know you.

B can also be for brainstorming, and this would be a creative, whiteboard session. Avoid making B for bitching, as you don't want to promote negative communication and mindset. If necessary, create V for venting because sometimes we need to get stuff off our chest, but limit the amount of time anybody has for this.

A is for advice. To get the best from people, it is advisable to let them know they can seek your advice if they are stuck or in doubt. Advice could take the form of coaching, a career conversation, or specific insights on project execution. Advice doesn't need to be in person; it can be by video call (Zoom, Teams), a phone call, or message channel (Slack, WhatsApp). You could use email, but I'm not a fan of using email for this purpose because it is too formal.

D is for decision. As a leader, there are decisions you will need to make and others that you have empowered your people or teams to make. When they come to you for a decision, how much prior information or briefing do you need to make the right decision? What channel or channels work best for you? Can this be done asynchronously, or do you need to be together in person?

I is for information. Who needs to know what and when? This is one of the biggest headaches for teams and organizations. The old operating system was to use a blind carbon copy (Bcc), which could be used passive-aggressively or to avoid responsibility. I highly recommend mapping out with your team what needs to be shared, with whom, when, and how. If you haven't already done this with your boss, then this is a conversation you also need to have.

In the online resource library, I have provided a worksheet for mapping out communication channels and decision-making processes to form the foundation of your Leadership Operating System (LOS). Check this out if you haven't already.

REFLECTION:

DO YOU KNOW HOW YOU OPERATE BEST?

DO YOU KNOW HOW YOUR TEAM OPERATES BEST?

HAVE YOU BEEN CLEAR WITH YOUR TEAM ABOUT HOW YOU WANT TO RUN MEETINGS, COMMUNICATION, AND DECISIONS?

SUMMARY FOR THE LEADERSHIP FRAMEWORK FOR DRIVING FOR ACCELERATED RESULTS

1. Management starts with setting clear expectations.
2. Fixed mindsets will pause progress as they seek perfection and don't take feedback well.
3. Motivation requires that people expect to improve, and improvement will reap relevant rewards.
4. Identify right behaviors and be able to describe them.
5. Validate right behaviors.
6. Choose the right channel for communication.
7. Know your BADI. What are you communicating with whom?
8. Map out a Leadership Operating System.

Part 3: The Plays

Play #1: The Why

At the end of the day, people follow those who know where they're going.

—Jack Trout

Just as the New Leadership Operating Framework begins by setting expectations, the first play focuses on setting expectations as to *why* any task or objective is important. The *why* is how leaders communicate how a task or project fits into the *big why*—the vision of the company—and the *small why*—why it matters to the person or people doing it.

Big 'Why' - Vision / Mission

Small 'Why' = What's important?
What's my purpose?

Figure 8: Big Why, Small Why

I recently polled my LinkedIn connections for why they do what they do.

Why do you do what you do?

For the money	**17%**
For the recognition	**2%**
For the satisfaction	**19%**
For the difference it makes	**62%**

Figure 9: Why do you do what you do?

It appears that over eighty percent of people do what they do for satisfaction and the difference it makes. This should not surprise us because these are the valence in Dr Vroom's Expectancy model, which I explained in Part 2.

A *why* frames mindset, which motivates and influences behavior. Here is a simple example. You:

a) ask an employee to drill a hole in the wall

b) explain that a picture needs to be hung on the wall to inspire the team, and the employee works out that they need to drill a hole to fix a hook for the picture.

Would the sense of satisfaction be greater in a) or b)?

When you are leading smart people with a sense of ownership, if you communicate the why, they can usually work out the what and the how. This doesn't mean what and how aren't necessary. You will often need to explain what a good result looks like, and if a person hasn't done something before, you will need to show them how. But *why* you do something is driven by a vision, and as a leader, you must have a clear vision for your team.

Start With Why (Sinek, 2011) makes the case that we should know why before what and how—understanding the reason why a task is necessary frames everything in terms of what the outcome will mean for us, our team, or our organization. This is crucial because, as humans, we are always searching for meaning.

The *big why* (vision) is a mental picture of the future. It is an idea and belief of what the future can hold. An effective vision also has a feeling. For example, what will it feel like to see this outcome in action?

REFLECTION:

THINK OF A TIME WHEN YOU WERE CRYSTAL CLEAR ABOUT WHY YOU WANTED TO ACHIEVE SOMETHING. REMEMBER HOW YOU PICTURED IT AND HOW YOU WOULD FEEL WHEN YOU ACHIEVED IT. NOW WRITE A SUMMARY OF THAT SCENARIO IN YOUR LEARNING DIARY.

There's a story about the early days of the computer and printer company Hewlett-Packard (HP). The team brainstormed their vision statement and came up with: 'To be the best design lab in the world'. An admirable objective, but it wasn't a vision their people could feel. So they changed 'in' to 'for', and the vision became: 'To be the best design lab for the world'. People then knew *why* they were working for HP.

REFLECTION:

WHEN SETTING EXPECTATIONS AS A LEADER, DO YOU TAKE THE TIME TO CONNECT THE TASK TO A SMALL WHY AND A BIG WHY?

Some years ago, a global bank asked if I would teach my leadership and self-leadership strategies to disadvantaged teenagers. The bank had partnered with a charity, which was the passionate creation of a wonderful but very private human being.

The bank provided a beautiful venue for the training and some willing volunteers to mentor the teenagers. My role was to facilitate an increase in self-esteem, self-confidence, communication, leadership skills, and equip the mentors with connection and coaching skills.

The first year was a steep learning curve, but I adapted to make the sessions fun and engaging for the teenagers and provide practical skills for the mentors. The following year, I was asked to repeat the program over a longer duration.

'I'd love to, but I'm not sure I can make the commitment as I will be busy with other projects.' I said.

'We'll pay your full fee.'

'I'm less busy.' I was curious why was the bank was so willing to commit funds.

The answer was the bank saw a significant return on this investment. Not only was this a corporate social responsibility project, but also the mentors had become super-engaged employees because they were contributing to something meaningful. Many of them had been promoted based on the coaching and leadership skills they had learned from me.

This is some of the most meaningful work I have ever done. I contributed to the program for five years and only stopped because I moved from Singapore to Portugal.

Sometimes our *why* is a cause-effect relationship from what we do. For example, a nurse sees the care and comfort they give to their patients. But sometimes, our meaning is orthogonal or tangential to our actions. A bee visits flowers to collect nectar, but as it does so, pollen is collected on the bristles of its legs, which results in the fertilization of flowers. The fertilization is tangential to the action of collecting nectar.

If I'm honest, I initially took the assignment with the disadvantaged teenagers because I wanted to build a relationship with the bank and do more consulting work. Tangentially, I found a massive reward in positively impacting the lives of a few hundred young people and became a better coach and human as a result.

> *If you hire people just because they can do a job, they work for your money. But if you hire people who believe what you believe, they will work for you with blood, sweat, and tears.*
>
> —Simon Sinek

When people work with *why*, the same time and effort yields a much bigger impact. This graphic illustrates this idea:

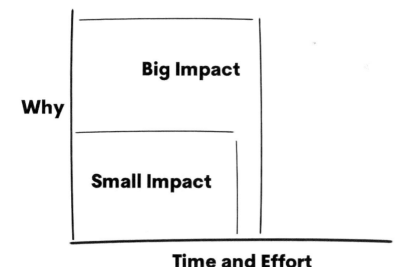

Figure 10: Why and Effort

USING THIS PLAY

Starting with *why* isn't reserved for ground-breaking visions; it is the foundation for all influence. For example, you might simply want your team to be punctual to meetings. You could tell them to be punctual, or you could explain why punctuality matters.

REFLECTION:
LIST FIVE OR MORE REASONS WHY PUNCTUALITY IS IMPORTANT:

Now, think about how you could frame your expectation in terms of *why*. Feel free to use the company's values or leadership principles. You could say: 'In terms of teamwork, it is important to show respect for your team member's time by showing up a few minutes before a scheduled meeting time and being prepared to contribute.'

REFLECTION:
YOUR TURN TO SET ANOTHER EXPECTATION USING WHY.

Communicating the *why* takes one of two forms:

- In terms of … (insert why), you need to do …

  Example: In terms of helping sales reach their quarter one goals, you need to provide a strong pipeline of qualified marketing leads.

- You need to do … because (insert why).

  Example: You need to develop a program for capturing and responding to product requests from customers because our lack of a program is causing customers to become frustrated with our brand.

The *why* should communicate excitement to help your team set positive expectations. In the second example above, the *why* is a negative (frustrated customers), but you can add the positive outcome of customers feeling more engaged and having more influence, resulting in happier customers and a stronger brand. It's important to communicate excitement because if you are not excited about the *why* your team won't be either.

The *why* should also challenge people to stretch their comfort zones, but not so much as to overwhelm them. The last thing anybody needs is another insurmountable task whose urgency level reads 'due yesterday.' Maybe in the first example above, a member of the marketing team could be asked to make a few cold calls to prospects to understand the sales experience.

Takeaway: the *why* should inspire people with a direction but not limit their freedom to choose how they get there. This is a difficult balance for leaders as they must walk a fine line between governance and guidance. Remember the sandbox metaphor for Dr Trompenaars that I shared in Part 1.

We each have the power to choose our frame of reference. Sometimes *why* creates passion, but sometimes it's driven by anger, frustration, or another emotion. Did you know that Uber was not started by two people passionate about transportation? It was started by two guys who came out of a conference in Paris and couldn't get a taxi. They were angry. 'This is ridiculous,' they said. 'There should be a way of organizing transportation!' And, right there, the idea behind Uber and the ride-sharing industry was created. The rest, as they say, is history.

PRACTICE:

START YOUR NEXT ONE-TO-ONE OR TEAM MEETING WITH WHY WHAT YOU ARE ABOUT TO SAY IS IMPORTANT FOR THE INDIVIDUAL/S AND FOR THE COMPANY (OR THE WORLD).

PLAY #2: OWNERSHIP

In the new organization, the worker is no longer a cog ... but is an intelligent part of the overall process.

—Bill Gates, 1999

'That's not my job.'

If you have been on the receiving end of this statement from a company representative, you will probably conclude that this person feels no ownership in their role.

If the person making this statement was part of your team, you would be mortified at the impact on customer service and seriously question their productivity.

As I have previously stated, it is my observation that the greatest challenge for a leader is to show empathy and hold people accountable. This play, in combination with Play #1: The Why, will go a long way towards meeting this challenge.

Ownership is built from responsibility and accountability, which are frequently used interchangeably, but I like to draw a distinction. Understanding this distinction will help you not just to deliver successful, high-quality outcomes but do so in an empathetic way.

Ownership

Responsible 'for'
- Your own mindset and actions
  - Finding options
- Taking opportunities
- Getting things done

Accountability 'to'
- Commitments/ Agreements made to self and others
- Values, Principles, and procedures

Figure 11: Responsibility and Accountability

A helpful way to think of these as distinct terms is understanding the boundary between what we are responsible *for* and what or who we are accountable *to* (Figure 11). For example, you can take ownership of building and distributing a report to your team. You are then responsible for delivering that report through capable methods and with acceptable quality, timeliness, and professionalism. However, you are accountable to your manager for delivering the report. If it fails to meet expectations, your manager will determine the consequences, such as more oversight and delayed advancement.

Responsibility for your thoughts, feelings, and actions in any given situation is the foundation of self-leadership, a principle we cover in Part 4: Leadership Principles.

Accountability is being held to account for following through on the commitments, duties, and responsibilities to ourselves and others.

Ownership is feeling in charge of delivering the desired outcome by understanding the *why* and executing the action.

Employees who feel this ownership will be more engaged and have a bias for action, resulting in greater agility, performance, and customer care. Therefore, as a leader, you must encourage ownership and avoid factors that reduce it, such as:

- micromanaging
- not delegating
- unclear expectations
- taking credit for employees' work
- blaming for issues out of a person's control
- not giving guidance or feedback
- allowing commitments to be missed.

Increasing ownership results from encouraging self-leadership, delegating effectively, giving regular feedback, and holding people accountable to commitments.

Holding People Accountable

In some delegation and project models, such as the RACI matrix, people or teams are tagged as being responsible, accountable, consulted, or informed. The owner of the work is designated as accountable and is responsible for ensuring the work is completed appropriately. Others are designated as responsible for doing the actual work. Accountability can be seen as an agreement on objectives and how to reach them, and the accountable person oversees and enforces compliance to a certain standard.

Accountability is best when standards are transparent and understood by all concerned. This is why accountability requires setting objectives, defining standards, and clearly explaining what is expected. People are either accountable or not based on their behaviors.

> When leading or coaching teams with self-leadership, it is essential to establish what behaviors are acceptable and what are not. (Bryant & Kazan, 2012)

The process of agreeing on acceptable behaviors is called 'norming' in teams (Tuckman, 1965). It can be likened to drawing a line. Above the line are the acceptable behaviors, and below it are the unacceptable ones.

Each team member should know the above-the-line and below-the-line behaviors, to which they will be held accountable. For example, a weekly status report can be unformatted and pasted into an email or created using the accepted template, which a manager has thoroughly explained. Employees should be held accountable for delivering their status reports with above-the-line behaviors, which means using the proper template in the proper format.

In Play #1: The Why, we looked at articulating the importance of punctuality. If a meeting is scheduled for 10 am, what time do you and each member of your team expect it to start? If the meeting doesn't start until all are present at 10.15 and no one is held accountable, the line has been set at 10.15.

To hold everybody accountable, encourage ownership, and give a *why*, you might say something like: 'As the manager responsible for this meeting, I would like to remind you that in terms of respect for all our time and for fostering teamwork, we come to meetings prepared, and our meetings begin on time. To not do so reflects badly on your ownership of time, diminishes your brand, and reduces the trust your colleagues place in you. Can you now commit to being punctual to these meetings?'

Using This Play

A great way to encourage people to take ownership, be responsible for themselves, and be accountable to the team's goals is through stories from your own experiences.

For example, like many major air carriers, Singapore Airlines is very procedural. Checklists create accountability. No matter how many years a flight attendant has flown, they will still read the take-off or landing instructions verbatim from a laminated card. And yet, with all this procedure, Singapore Airlines staff are very good at taking ownership.

During the SARS crisis of 2003, an incident occurred, and the Singaporean government instructed Changi Airport to be locked down. This meant passengers at departure gates would be locked in and unable to leave. When Singapore Airlines staff realized this, they ran to all the food outlets in the airport, using their own money to buy whatever food they could. They handed this food to passengers as the gate doors were sealed.

This action was driven by the Singapore Airlines staff taking ownership of the challenge and solving it on their own. The passengers were likely very grateful that the Singapore Airlines staff didn't wait for a non-existent manual to arrive. They just acted.

My sixteen-year-old daughter understands ownership and responsibility. We are currently in different countries, so to stay connected, I have been playing Minecraft with her on the computer. I asked her to help me enchant some armor, as she is experienced and I am the noob.

'I could do it for you,' she said, 'but then you wouldn't learn anything.'

I was so proud. I am always talking about ownership and responsibility, and now my daughter was teaching me!

REFLECTION:

WHAT IS A STORY THAT YOU CAN TELL ABOUT OWNERSHIP?

Takeaway: Ownership gives people power to control their destiny whilst, signaling that you trust them to deliver on the expectations. But ownership comes with accountability, and managers must hold their teams accountable for their behaviors, actions, and ownership.

PRACTICE:

IN YOUR NEXT INTERACTION WITH YOUR TEAM, CHECK THE LEVEL OF OWNERSHIP THEY FEEL OVER THE TASKS THEY HAVE BEEN DELEGATED.

Play #3: Feedback

There is no failure. Only feedback.

—Robert Allen

Having covered The Why and Ownership, it would seem logical to talk about objectives. Instead, I want to talk about feedback because knowing how to give feedback will make you better at setting objectives and reduce the amount of feedback you will need to give. Follow me?

Once a goal or objective is set, your people will use their behaviors, experiences, learnings, and more to work towards that goal. But what do we do if they don't hit the target or are clearly off course?

You will need to provide feedback if members of your team fall short or struggle on the path to their objective. Feedback closes the gap between behavior and objective and gives people information about how they are doing. It occurs when a behavior (what is said and done) is observed and played back in a sensory way to the performer.

For feedback to be effective, it must be measured against an articulated target or objective, which we'll cover in the next play, Objective Setting. If you didn't effectively communicate an objective, you can't give effective feedback. This would just be criticism. Done well, a feedback conversation will improve mindset and performance. Done poorly, it can demoralize and result in further disruptions to performance.

Feedback is, without doubt, the biggest leverage for increasing human performance and company results.

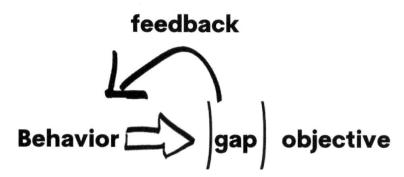

Figure 12: Feedback

Delivering Feedback

Many people perceive feedback as criticism, so you must set the intention that you are giving feedback for growth, not to blame or rescue. Remember to be empathetic, not judgmental. Make your feedback about observed behavior and do it as soon as possible after witnessing that behavior.

Good feedback offers specific details on what you observed. Ask the person about their intention and explore if they understand the behavior, recognize the impact, and know how to self-correct.

The goal is to communicate that there is no failure, only feedback for improvement.

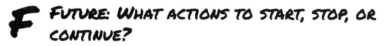

Figure 13: The FIF Model

The FIF model helps frame your feedback—positive or negative—for growth. It helps you focus on the facts of the observation, the impact, and the future adjustments to be made. Using this model, you can have regular, short conversations that are well received.

Facts

Feedback starts by stating the facts, so you have a shared reality with the person. You can't give feedback if the person doesn't recognize the facts, so this step ensures ownership is established.

Imagine Stephen, who is competent in his role but tends to keep to himself, although his peers seek his opinion and seem to trust his advice. You have noticed that despite his competence and trust-worthiness, Stephen keeps quiet in meetings and doesn't offer his perspectives.

> Here's how you might state the facts to Stephen:
>
> 'Hi, Steven, I wanted to speak with you about the meeting we just had and your behavior in other meetings over the last few weeks.
>
> 'Stephen, we were discussing a topic in your area of expertise and responsibility, but you did not offer an opinion. I have noticed that you have kept quiet in other meetings as well. It seems this is a pattern. Do you agree?'

Impact

The next step in the FIF model is to establish the impact of the individual's behavior, and you could inquire about their intention behind the behavior. You can't offer constructive feedback without understanding the person's intention or jumping to a conclusion.

The impact of Steven not speaking up in meetings includes vital insights that are not considered, and his personal brand is non-existent. You could tell this to Steven, or you could help him realize it himself.

> 'Realizing you are knowledgeable on the topic, Steven, I'm curious about your intention to stay quiet.'
>
> Stephen: 'Well, I guess I don't like to speak out of turn.'
>
> 'There's no hierarchy in these meetings. If you don't speak up when you have insights, how do you think that might impact the project?'

Notice the use of questions to establish intention and impact. To adjust behavior, the person receiving the feedback must take ownership. They are more likely to do so if they come up with the answers.

As a manager, always assume a positive intention behind any behavior. The employee does what they do because it has an internal logic for them. It is important to make the employee aware of the impact of that behavior, good or bad.

> **REFLECTION:**
>
> DO YOU ASSUME POSITIVE INTENTION, OR DO YOU GET ANGRY THAT PEOPLE DON'T EXACTLY BEHAVE AS YOU THINK THEY SHOULD?

Future

Once the worker is aware of the impact, you can help adjust their positive intention to create a different future behavior that gets the right outcome. For example:

> 'Stephen, your opinion matters. If you keep quiet in meetings, it not only impacts the project but also reduces your visibility, which will impact your prospects for promotion.'
>
> Stephen: 'Well, if you put it that way.'
>
> 'I believe you are a valuable member of the team, and I know your peers value your opinion. What do you think you can do better in the future?'

If possible, avoid prescribing or dictating the new behavior. Ask the person to describe what they will do to get closer to the target. Ask, 'What are you going to stop, start, or continue to do in the future?'

> 'Stephen, in terms of improving your impact, what do you think you should do?'
>
> Stephen: 'I will make an effort to be more assertive in meetings.'
>
> 'Great! When will we witness this new behavior?'
>
> Stephen: 'At our next meeting, I will give my input.'
>
> 'That's great, Stephen. I'm looking forward to your contribution.'

USING THIS PLAY

You will likely use this play every day you have contact with the people you lead. You can also use it in conversations with peers and, in certain circumstances, your own manager.

The One Minute Manager (Blanchard & Johnson, 1994) is a management classic. The first principle is a one-minute conversation that includes what good behaviors look like to set expectations. The second principle is one-minute praising, focusing on specific behaviors. The third is the one-minute correction to provide feedback on behaviors that are not working.

FIF works equally well for validating behaviors that work and don't work. It provides a perfect model for this because it's important to let people know that you are not criticizing them but correcting behaviors to achieve goals.

Remember that to be an effective leader, you need to articulate what good and bad behaviors look, sound, and feel like. You must also communicate via tone and body language that the feedback is for growth, not criticism.

Immediate and accurate feedback is a gift to the person receiving it. Never hold back thinking you are being nice. Being nice is a behavior we teach our children, and as adults, we like it when people are nice to us. So what is so wrong with being nice?

If you value being considerate, pleasant, friendly, and well-mannered, then, by all means, behave that way and encourage others to do the same. But it may surprise you that being nice does not mean these things.

The etymology of the word nice is from the Latin *nescius*, meaning ignorant; in Old French, *nescire*, meaning 'not know'; and in Middle English, it meant stupid. The ignorance in being nice is not knowing how to be disagreeable or to give feedback without causing offence. The harm this does to you and your career is the inability to be honest. It's natural to want to be liked, but being nice can get in the way of communicating important challenges and opportunities.

Being nice does not help your people grow.

PRACTICE:

THIS WEEK, GIVE POSITIVE OR NEGATIVE FEEDBACK TO ONE OF YOUR TEAM MEMBERS.

PLAY #4: OBJECTIVE SETTING

It is not enough to take steps which may someday lead to a goal; each step must be itself a goal and a step likewise.

—Johann Wolfgang Von Goethe

This book is about delivering accelerated results, and this requires setting clear objectives. An objective or goal is something planned for the future. A key component of objective and goal setting is setting expectations, which we explored in Part 2: The Leadership Framework. Setting expectations frames mindsets, and mindsets inform behaviors.

Why is objective setting important? It is unlikely that our actions and behaviors will be effective if we don't know the objective. It is impossible to have a fully engaged mindset if we don't know what we're moving towards. And what we're working towards is our objective.

For an objective to be engaging, it should describe what people will see, hear, and feel when they achieve it. The SMART process reminds you to communicate objectives so they are specific, measurable, attainable, relevant, and time bound.

S Specific

m Measurable

A Attainable

r Relevant

T Time Bound

Humans are conscious beings, so we constantly imagine ourselves in a future state. By being specific with that imagination, we can effectively navigate our actions to arrive at our desired destination.

When you have specific objectives, you can plan, organize, work with others, and delay immediate gratification for future rewards. With a clear goal, you can say yes to what is important and no to anything that doesn't matter or is a distraction.

In 1954, Peter Drucker introduced Managing by Objectives (MBOs), and Andy Grove (Intel) further developed this idea into the OKR framework, which is popular with software companies, such as Google.

O is for Objective. Objectives should be significant, concrete, action-oriented, and (ideally) inspirational. When properly designed and deployed, they eliminate all confusion.

KR is for Key Results. Key results benchmark and monitor how the objective is accomplished. Effective KRs are specific and time-bound, aggressive yet realistic. Most of all, they are measurable and verifiable. You either meet a key result's requirements, or you don't. There is no grey area and no room for doubt. At the end of a designated period, typically a quarter, managers should check in on the results and grade them as fulfilled or not.

OKRs are being integrated into productivity tools. For example, in 2021 Microsoft acquired Ally.io, planning to add Ally's OKR tracking and dashboard to Microsoft's Teams communication software.

Objectives are strongly linked to our motivation, which is linked to agency. Agency is the feeling that we control our behaviors, and our behaviors make a difference. Conversely, objectives over which we feel little or no agency quickly lead to demotivation, which is similar to the demotivation that occurs when we don't know why an objective has been set.

REFLECTION: RECALL A GOAL YOU ACHIEVED.

ON A SCALE OF 1 TO 10 (1 BEING NO AGENCY AND 10 BEING COMPLETE AGENCY), HOW MUCH AGENCY (CONTROL) DID YOU FEEL OVER THE OUTCOME?

1 2 3 4 5 6 7 8 9 10

> Do you feel like you are driving, or are you just a
> passenger on a bus going nowhere?

It is important to convey agency when setting objectives for your team. Don't just tell people their objectives. Engage them in co-creating objectives they feel ownership of. This is the self-leadership approach, or the practice of intentionally influencing your thinking, feeling, and actions towards your objectives.

Effective objective setting links what the person wants to achieve with what the organization needs or wants. This is the *why*.

People pursue and achieve objectives when they perceive agency over their actions.

When we explored mindset, we learned that people are motivated to pursue objectives when they believe the process of taking action (effort) will increase performance.

People pursue objectives when they value their future self who will achieve this objective; the objective is then relevant.

A simple example of the above would be going to the gym with the goal of improving fitness. You have agency because you control your decision to go to the gym and exercise. You believe the behavior of lifting weights will improve your strength (performance), which is confirmed over time. You pursue your objective because you imagine yourself physically stronger.

Expectancy theory shows you can set *process* and *outcome* objectives.

The *process* of getting fit is within your control because you choose the behavior of regularly going to the gym and lifting weights.

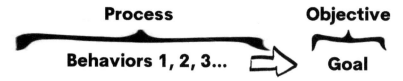

Figure 14: Process and Objectives

The *outcome* of these actions—maybe to gain five kilograms of muscle by a specific date—is the objective. However, this may not be 100 percent within your control. Your metabolism or an injury could prevent you from reaching the objective by the date.

Setting only *outcome* objectives can lead to demotivation if circumstances, not effort, prevent reaching the objective. Similarly, setting only *process* goals can lead to the process being the proxy or excuse, where managers who fail to reach targets say: 'But I followed procedure.'

An experienced leader sets both process and
outcome goals and constantly reviews the process
to ensure it is effective.

REFLECTION:
THINK OF A CURRENT OBJECTIVE. WHAT IS THE OUTCOME?
WHAT PROCESS (BEHAVIORS) ARE YOU USING TO ACHIEVE
THE GOAL? WHAT ADJUSTMENTS, IF ANY, NEED TO BE MADE
TO THE PROCESS?

As a leader, your job is to orchestrate a team of extraordinary people that together can accomplish what you could not do alone.

—Jim Whitehurst, President at
IBM and former CEO of Red Hat.

Using This Play

Setting goals and achieving objectives are core to delivering accelerated results. So, when writing the play, I doubted whether I would be sharing anything new. Until I had an initial coaching session with a partner in one of the big professional service firms, let's call the partner Francois. Francois' boss was leaving in a few months, and he was taking over the entire function for the region.

Normally, I would start a coaching session by clarifying the goals for the coaching and where a person would like to be in the next four to six months, but I picked up that Francois was uncomfortable with something. He confessed that he struggled with procrastination and was experiencing a level of impostor syndrome about being a leader. I discuss more about impostor syndrome in the next play, Confidence.

If you experience self-doubt, you will significantly reduce your chances of achieving your objectives. Yes, goals can be big and scary, but you must believe you can achieve them, even if it requires a lot of work and commitment.

I asked Francois what he loved to do, and he shared that he plays the saxophone and enjoys solving software problems. This information enabled me to confirm with Francois that he has a history of following through (learning to play the saxophone), and that developing his leadership skills is like solving a software problem. With the objective reframed and Francois able to let go of negative self-talk, we talked about the goal. As a summary, here are the steps to successful objective setting:

- Make objectives as specific as possible using SMART or OKRs.
- Ensure each person knows their responsibilities (agency).
- Articulate deliverables in terms of time, quantity, and quality (accountability).
- Visualize achieving the objective with the team (why).
- Where possible, discuss objectives with the team to get buy-in (ownership).
- Once objectives are set, keep everybody on track through feedback.

> **PRACTICE:**
>
> **WHAT OBJECTIVES HAVE YOU SET FOR YOUR TEAM?**
> **HAVE YOU FOLLOWED ALL THE STEPS ABOVE?**

PLAY #5: CONFIDENCE

Confidence is the mindset of being certain of your abilities or having trust in people, plans, or the future. When building confidence, the first person to trust is yourself. Confidence is key to everything you do as a manager. You must be confident in your decisions and actions, but it's also important that you develop confidence in your people.

Experience leads to confidence. If you have accomplished a task in the past, or something similar, you can trust your ability to repeat it. If you are doing something you've never done, but believe in your ability to work it out, take feedback, and learn, this is a special type of confidence called self-efficacy.

Confidence is not walking into a room,
thinking you are better than somebody else. Confidence
is walking into a room, knowing you don't have to
compare yourself with anybody else.

Encouraging Confidence

As a manager or leader, delivering results is key to your success, but encouraging people to be the best version of themselves to deliver those results will be your legacy.

Peter is a director at one of the Big Four accounting firms. He is an introvert who prefers to let his work speak for itself. A few years ago, Peter and I did some coaching together, where I helped him project his confidence and gravitas, his executive presence.

Peter has re-engaged me to help him align the *big why* of his firm with his own purpose, the *small why*. As we probed what made Peter happy at work, we discovered that he loved the small interactions with younger employees. It turns out that Peter's purpose is to make sure there are more competent people in leadership positions, but the competent people are often overlooked because they don't project confidence.

Confident people who lack competency often suffer from the Dunning Kruger cognitive bias (Kruger & Dunning, 1999). They simply don't know what they don't know but think highly of themselves regardless.

Such people require feedback or a difficult conversation. This play is not for them; it is for those who are competent or developing their competence but lack confidence. These people often run a pattern of discounting their achievements or suffer from impostor syndrome.

Impostor syndrome is a psychological pattern in which an individual doubts their skills, talents, or accomplishments and has a persistent internalized fear of being exposed as a fraud. An example would be a new employee assuming they were at a disadvantage because they were new to a company or role. They might keep quiet during meetings, always strive for perfection, and assume others knew more than they did. They repeatedly discount themselves, which saps their self-belief and slows their progress.

A huge amount of intellectual capital is lost in meetings because people don't have the confidence to speak up and share their ideas. It could be due to low self-esteem or a cultural issue that prevents one from a person from wanting to stand out. This typically comes with an internal dialogue that goes something like, *You're new to this company, so what do you know?* Or, *I don't know these people yet. They might be smarter than me, so I'd better keep quiet.*

Using this Play

The growth mindset, which we discussed previously, is key to coaching confidence. You need to help your people understand that they don't need to be perfect to be confident, but they do need to be confident to progress. Waiting for full competence to be confident is foolhardy, but everyone can learn to take on the posture of confidence, the breathing of confidence, the narrative of confidence, and project confidence

Sports coaches and athletes understand that confidence positively impacts performance. So they engage in rituals or strategies to ensure mind and body are aligned before they run the race or play the game.

Use this 3A strategy to coach yourself and your people to be more confident.

 ACCESS (REMEMBER) A TIME YOU FELT 100% CONFIDENT DOING SOMETHING. CHOOSE SOMETHING SIMPLE LIKE RIDING A BIKE OR MAKING INSTANT NOODLES.

 AMPLIFY THIS FEELING IN YOUR BODY. NOTICE THE POSTURE OF CONFIDENCE, THE BREATHING. NOW BECOME AWARE OF WHAT IT'S LIKE TO LOOK OUT THROUGH THE EYES OF CONFIDENCE.

 ADD OR EDIT AN INNER NARRATIVE THAT REINFORCES THIS CONFIDENCE. FOR EXAMPLE: "I AM CONFIDENT AND CAN HANDLE WHATEVER COMES MY WAY."

Figure 15: Confidence Play

Most people think confidence follows competence, but the 3A strategy accesses confidence before even thinking about competency. For example, before giving a presentation, a person can spend hours preparing a slide deck and worrying about what questions might be asked. Or they can access confidence through the 3As and prepare the content to the best of their ability. The content is more likely to positively influence the audience if delivered from a confident physiology than an anxious one.

> **NOTE: CONFIDENCE ALLOWS US TO SHOWCASE COMPETENCE; IT IS NOT A SUBSTITUTE FOR IT. YOU STILL NEED TO KNOW YOUR STUFF AND PRACTICE YOUR SKILL.**

Poi Toong works for a US Fortune 500 industrial automation company and is responsible for leading the channel business across Southeast Asia. Poi Toong would lose his confidence and get intimidated presenting to big personalities, even though he had twenty-five years of experience.

'I believe I have competency to do what I'm good at,' he told me. 'But I don't feel that I'm complete—something is missing. My inner narrative is telling me that I'm not ready, or I do not deserve to be who I am today. This makes me frustrated and sad.'

His struggle was real, and it was negatively impacting his career prospects as his lack of confidence had him labeled as lightweight.

I helped Poi Toong change his inner narrative and practice the 3A strategy. The result was a transformation.

'I am now feeling confident and acknowledged. I get positive feedback on points that I share. I am no longer afraid to be vulnerable, even in front of senior leaders. I am okay to say I don't know if I genuinely don't know.'

As you use this play, you will become more confident in identifying and reframing inner narratives. Play #12: Coaching will also help.

Here are some confidence-building narratives to get you started:

- I am valuable; I am capable.
- I am confident in my ability to handle what comes my way.
- My ideas and perspectives add value, and I will share them.
- I own my confidence, regardless of who is in the room.

Sometimes, what we label as a lack of self-confidence is actually a symptom of low self-esteem. The difference is that low confidence comes from doubting you can do it, whereas low self-esteem comes from thinking you are not worthy of doing it. This lack of self-worth usually has roots in unfavorable comparisons with real or imagined perfection.

A mantra that has worked wonders for many of my clients is:

I have nothing to prove, only things to improve.

The power of this phrase is that it taps into the growth mindset and sets us up to try new things. Will you say it to yourself for the next few days? Trust me! You won't regret it.

PRACTICE:

IDENTIFY SOMEONE IN YOUR TEAM WHO COULD INCREASE THEIR LEVEL OF CONFIDENCE. HELP THEM TO ACCESS, AMPLIFY, AND ADD TO THEIR INNER NARRATIVE.

PLAY #6: COLLABORATION

If you want to go fast, go alone. If you want to go far, go together.

—African Proverb

Collaboration is essential to accelerate results and scale your team or company. The behavior of working with others (in person or virtually) to produce something is the nature of business. It's rare that anyone does everything as an individual contributor. Usually, we are part of a team or an organization.

> Collaboration is employees communicating and working together, building on each other's ideas to produce something new or do something differently. A collaborative organization unlocks the potential, capacity, and knowledge of every employee, thereby generating value, innovation and improving productivity in its workplace. (Deloitte, 2014, p. 4)

The absence of collaboration is expensive in terms of inefficiencies and lost opportunities, and the emotional cost of frustration from internal politics is immeasurable.

I once heard an HR director at Timberland say, 'You train dogs; you develop people.' This has stuck with me ever since. So, when I was asked to run conflict management training for a software company in Singapore, I explained to the client that giving people conflict management strategies is a great idea, but the conflict would remain unless the underlying causes of the conflict were addressed.

'Who is in conflict with whom, and about what?' I asked.

With more gentle probing, I discovered that the engineering team was motivated and rewarded to keep the servers online and secure. The innovation team was motivated and rewarded for developing new solutions and selling them to market.

'I'm curious,' I probed further. 'Does the innovation team need to test their beta software on the engineering team's servers?'

The answer was 'yes', and this was the source of the conflict because if the innovation team's product wasn't perfect, it had a negative impact on the engineering team's key performance indicators. With this information, I suggested a program for collaboration to prevent any further conflict.

An employee has a problem with a colleague from another department, but rather than collaborating, they escalate it to their boss, who escalates it to their boss, who speaks to his colleague in the other department, who speaks to his direct report, who speaks with the employee, who explains why it can't be done. Does this sound familiar?

Despite the many benefits of collaboration, including flexibility, engagement, innovation, alignment, and speed, we often find people working alone, in silos, or in conflict.

This play is about overcoming barriers to collaboration and establishing a mindset where collaboration is the norm rather than internal competition.

Barriers to collaboration include:

- weak egos—driving a need for power over others
- lack of confidence—causing people to not communicate
- fear of consequences—leading to people keeping ideas to themselves
- an ill-designed reward system—creating competition between people and departments

- out of date procedures—resulting in process over people
- unwillingness to consider other's perspectives—driving ignorance and arrogance.

Your role as a leader is to create an environment where people feel safe to contribute and collaborate. You can do this by role modeling, humility, assertive communication, and setting clear roles and responsibilities.

Modeling Humility

Many people and cultures value humility, but in my experience, humility is often misunderstood and applied.

The word humility derives from the Latin word *humilitas*, which can be translated as 'humble', or as 'grounded' or 'from the earth' since it derives from *humus* (earth).

Collaboration works best when people are grounded in their sense of self and their skills.

From a positive psychology standpoint (Tangney 2002), humility is:

- Having an accurate, neither over nor underestimated, view of your abilities.
- Being able to accept other people's perspectives as equally valid as your own.

The first point speaks to self-leadership—having healthy self-esteem and self-confidence. We want to collaborate with people who know their stuff.

In 2021, I had a health scare just before my sixtieth birthday. The details are on selfleadership.com/blog, but to cut a long story short, a surgeon told me that he would need to remove a third of my colon.

'Are you any good at this procedure?' I asked.

He was surprised by my question but responded, 'I recently spent a year in the USA studying and practicing this procedure. So yes, I am good at it.'

This was the answer I was looking for because if he had hesitated or responded with false humility, I would have looked for another surgeon.

We want to collaborate with people who are good at what they do. So, as a leader, encourage your people to say 'I'm good at X' and back that up with evidence.

The second point—to accept other people's perspectives as equally valid as your own—is the key to collaboration and, ultimately, creativity. Listening openly and without being defensive is often a learned skill. Sometimes, we need to learn this by unlearning the biases and prejudices we have picked up during our lives.

I regularly recommend my coachees take an introductory improvisation (improv) theatre class. The first rule of improv is saying 'Yes, and …' The second rule of improv is to make your partner look good.

In improv, a player might start a story or action, and another player will build on that action by saying, 'Yes, and ...' For example, player one starts the story with 'I woke up one morning and I was wearing roller skates in bed'. Now, this is improbable and a bit strange; however, this would not phase an improv player who would build on the story with 'Yes, and there was an ostrich pecking at my toes'. And so, the story builds.

In contrast, we could respond with, 'That's stupid, you would have woken up when you rolled over unless you were very drunk.' This response would be judgmental, make the storyteller look bad, and not be creative. This is called 'Yes, but' behavior.

If I were to say 'I really like you, but …', You would immediately be defensive because the 'but' had just discounted the preceding, 'I really like you'. If I instead said, 'I really like you, and …', you would more likely be open and curious.

You are probably familiar with the swear jar, where people must put in a dollar every time they cuss. Well, let me introduce you to a 'but jar'.

When you lead meetings, try setting the rule that there are no 'buts', and if people persist, you will instigate a 'but jar', which will be donated to charity when full. This is a fun example of team norming that we discussed earlier and a good way to foster collaborative communication.

Instead of hearing 'I like your idea, but I disagree', you will start hearing things like 'That's a great contribution and here is a way to make it even better'.

The second rule of improv is to make your partner look good, which breeds a psychological safety where people are free to say and try new things without fear of reprisal.

CHALLENGE:

I'D LIKE YOU TO GO ON A 'BUT' DIET. REMOVE 'BUT' FROM YOUR VOCABULARY EXCEPT WHEN EXPRESSLY NEGATING THE PREVIOUS IDEA. FOR THE NEXT TWENTY-ONE DAYS, RESPOND TO ANY INQUIRY WITH A VERSION OF, 'YES, AND …'
ARE YOU UP FOR THE CHALLENGE?

Assertive Communication

Effective collaboration requires a mindset shift from competition to abundance and from solution first to needs first.

> **LET ME ILLUSTRATE WITH A SIMPLE THOUGHT EXPERIMENT: IMAGINE TWO TEENAGE SISTERS, LET'S CALL THEM LOUISE AND DENISE. LOUISE AND DENISE EACH WANT AN ORANGE AND PROCEED TO THE KITCHEN. WHEN THEY ARRIVE, THEY DISCOVER THERE IS ONLY ONE ORANGE LEFT.**
>
> **WHAT DO THEY DO?**

I have posed this question to many groups around the world, and the immediate answer is usually to cut the orange in half. Other solutions include substituting the orange, fighting over the orange, or buying another.

I ask whether cutting the orange in half is a win-win.

Many people will tell me 'yes' and are surprised when I disagree and inform them that getting fifty percent of what you want is not a win-win but a compromise.

So, how do we collaborate for a win-win outcome? Well, do we know what Louise needs the orange for? Do we know what Denise needs the orange for? Or were we in such a hurry to get to a solution that we forgot to ask?

Perhaps, Louise needs the orange for an orange cake, and Denise needs the orange for juice. If this was the case, Louise only needs the orange skin, which leaves Denise with the orange flesh for her juice—a win-win!

Louise and Denise are both part of the same family, so collaboration is preferable to conflict. Working for an organization is like being in a family. We have individual and departmental needs to achieve our objectives, but so do our colleagues in other departments.

So, collaboration starts with an inquiry to needs, such as: 'What's important to you about that?'

This curiosity comes from the win-win mindset and that nobody matters more than the whole.

To encourage collaboration in your teams, make sure your people are clear about what they need and what others need.

If we only know what we need, want, or believe, our communication and behaviors are aggressive. If we only know what others need, want, or believe, our communication and behaviors are passive (see Figure 16).

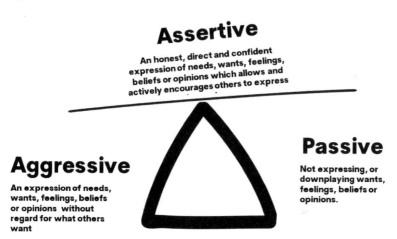

Figure 16: Assertive Communication

Assertive communication allows different perspectives to be heard and resolved because it is an honest, direct, and confident expression of needs, wants, feelings, beliefs, or opinions, which allows and actively encourages others to express themselves.

As a leader, you can model assertive communication and coach your team members to get better at identifying their own needs and the needs of others. You will know you have achieved this because you will hear things like: 'OK, I understand you need X and believe we should do Y. I've asked for A and want to do B. Let's work together so we both get what we want and move this forward.'

Roles and Responsibilities

> Effective expectation setting is key
> to efficient collaboration.

Using what we have learned about ownership, we can apply the 'Responsible For/Accountable To' model to create a foundation for effective collaboration and conflict management.

Everyone is responsible for themselves and accountable for shared goals and agreed behaviors.

> A champion team will always beat a team of champions.

Managers need to discuss and decide on roles and responsibilities without being prescriptive. Knowing exactly who is responsible, what they are accountable for, who to consult, and who to inform at every step will significantly improve your chances of success. Luckily for us, the responsibility assignment matrix (RACI) can help track this whilst preventing people from saying, 'That's not my job.'

RACI stands for responsible, accountable, consulted, and informed. It describes the participation of individuals in working towards an objective as follows:

Responsible: People or stakeholders who do the work. They must complete the task or objective and make the decision. Several people can be jointly responsible.

Accountable: An accountable person signs approval when a shared goal is met. Success requires that there is only one person accountable, which means 'the buck stops here'.

Consulted: People or stakeholders who need to give input before the work can be started or completed are consulted for their input. These people are active participants and are frequently updated.

Informed: People or stakeholders who need to be kept up to date on progress or findings are informed. They may need updates on decisions, roadblocks, or information, but they do not need to be formally consulted or contribute directly to a task or decision.

A RACI matrix details the individuals in each of the above roles, so there is no confusion.

An example was the rebranding of Host Analytics to Planful in 2020. This project required collaboration between Marketing, Finance, Legal, and the CEO. It was a big project with a short time span, but everybody knew why it was important and their role in making it to completion.

Step	Project Initiation	CEO	SVP Marketing	Legal	Comms Manager	Marketing Manager
1	Develop New Branding Guide	A	R	C	I	I
2	Rebrand Website	I	A	I	C	R
3	Rebrand Collateral	I	A	I	C	R
4	Communicate Rebranding	C	A	I	R	I

Collaboration builds trust and inclusivity

Initially, we might trust somebody because of their position, qualifications, or reputation, but real trust is built working alongside someone in the trenches. In *The Five Dysfunctions of a Team*, (2002) Patrick Lencioni writes that people need trust to have effective conflict. Working through the conflict, we gain commitment, and with commitment, we gain accountability and results.

Collaboration is not without conflict, but when we trust the intentions and capabilities of our team members, we can work through the conflict to find robust solutions we can commit to.

Using this Play

I know of no single formula for success. But over the years I have observed that some attributes of leadership are universal and are often about finding ways of encouraging people to combine their efforts, their talents, their insights, their enthusiasm and their inspiration to work together.

—Queen Elizabeth II

When I think of collaboration, I always get the mental image of a rural community building a barn for one of its members. A barn is too big to build by yourself, so you get your neighbors to help you. In turn, when they need a barn, you go to their farm and help.

Using this play requires role modeling, collaboration, and encouraging your team to leverage their efforts by collaborating in turn. Be vigilant for any kind of silo thinking or turf-marking, and nip this behavior in the bud by holding people accountable to this leadership principle.

PRACTICE:

IF YOU ARE NOT CURRENTLY COLLABORATING, LOOK FOR AN OPPORTUNITY TO DO SO.

IF YOU ARE COLLABORATING, ASSERTIVELY COMMUNICATE TO MAKE THE COLLABORATION BETTER.

PLAY #7: CAREER CONVERSATIONS

A single conversation across the table with a wise man is better than ten years' mere study of books.

—Henry Wadsworth Longfellow

Karin was frustrated. She felt taken for granted and knew she was being under-compensated. What added insult to injury was that her manager made no attempt to engage her about what she wanted, despite her driving one of the biggest and most complicated technology projects in the company's history.

Karin confided in me that she had started to look outside her firm because she didn't feel recognized and was not being recompensed for the impact she was making.

How many good talents, like Karin, are lost to companies because nobody took the time to have a career conversation and find out what's important?

You might feel like Karin, but as a manager, you need to make sure you are not losing good people because you didn't run this play.

As it turns out, I was able to help Karin frame the conversation with her manager and, at the time of writing, she is getting acknowledgment for the work she is doing and is in line for a salary bump.

Career conversations are not performance reviews and are not necessarily about a pay rise. They are about utilizing talents and developing skills. The strength and sustainability of a company depends on attracting, retaining, and developing good talent, and career conversations are a vital part of this. Considering the importance of these conversations, many managers feel at a loss on how to have them, often because they did not receive good conversations themselves.

We have already discussed the benefits of feedback in Play #3: Feedback Conversations. By regularly framing feedback using the fact–impact–future (FIF) model, you will provide clarity about current performance and future improvement. However, for this conversation, the focus is on the individual's career.

There are two important aspects of career progression in any company:

- What the *worker* wants to develop and achieve.
- What the *company* needs in terms of talent.

I work closely with Rahul Kalia, Global Head of Culture and Transformation for Bayer. One day, Rahul was having a career conversation with a high potential from the marketing department in the Asia-Pacific region. The manager was thirty-seven years old and said, 'If I don't get a promotion by next year, I won't be able to hit my goal to be at a certain level by forty-nine.' This was a typical conversation with an ambitious person from this part of the world, and Rahul had just the right advice.

'You are from marketing, so you are familiar with the Ansoff Matrix (CFI Education Inc, 2022), a two by two grid that looks at new and existing markets and products. Well, replace market with skills and product with experience. Now map where you have most engaged.'

I have created this matrix in Figure 17—Kalia's Career Matrix.

Figure 17: Kalia's Career Matrix

The high potential realized, he was most happy and engaged when developing new skills within his existing experience (the learning zone). Rahul advised him to look around the company for roles that met these criteria. As it happened, such a role did not yet exist, but it was created when this individual identified a need and contributed to solving the need.

Frame a career conversation around progression, not promotion or pay. It is about the individual's growth within the organization— what the individual wants, balanced with what the company needs.

We have previously talked about how people are motivated when they feel they have control. They want to feel their efforts will improve performance, and that performance needs to be meaningful to them. A career conversation allows the worker to make the mental and emotional connection between the targets they have been set and their own career growth and progress. Reinforce the point that the worker has ownership over their career, and your role is to support their progress. As the manager, you have more visibility into what is possible for your people, and you can expand this visibility with conversations with your manager and human resources (people and culture).

A career conversation doesn't have to be a formal, sit-down affair. It can be a short meeting over coffee, in person or virtually. Let the person know that you want to talk about their career, and you schedule these conversations with everyone on your team.

Birch wood is used extensively in construction, so use this BIRCH to construct a great career conversation:

B   Be present and actively listen to how the individual wants to develop.

I   Invite the individual to talk about what engages them & gives them energy.

R   Reflect on what has already been achieved, and areas you see for future growth.

C   Contextualize how contributions & skills help the company's current & future needs

H   Help them with resources and people they may learn from. Set up ongoing conversations.

Figure 18: Career Conversations

Be present and actively listen because an effective career conversation requires you to understand how the individual wants to develop.

Invite the individual to talk about what energizes and motivates them. Ask questions to expand on what engages and stretches their affinities and skills.

Reflect on what has already been achieved and point out areas where there is room for future growth. It's very important to anchor how far somebody has already come. Point out what they've learned since joining your team and where they might want to continue growing.

Contextualize how contributions and skills help the company's current and future needs. By connecting the dots between their skills and what the company needs, you create a feeling of belonging and certainty for the worker and encourage them to seek opportunities for learning and growth.

Help them with resources. You might not have all the answers, but you have connections to people who can help. The worker's future growth might not be in your department, or they might need to get experience elsewhere. Think beyond your immediate need from the worker and, instead, think that your legacy will be the subtle influence you have on another's career.

It's Not All About Pay

Money is only one way of keeping score; there are other ways. Workers also want validation, acknowledgment, growth, learning, and influence. Every worker is a holistic person who needs to grow in multiple dimensions. It's your job to help them connect the dots from where they are to where they want to go.

Using This Play

Here are three career conversation examples for how to use this play:

I Want a Raise

During a discussion, a team member says, 'I've been here a year and worked really hard. I've learned a lot and done what you asked me to do; I think it's time for a pay rise.' You may or may not be privy to whether this person could have a pay rise now, and you could find out. But remember, the career conversation is about more than just money.

Using BIRCH, you could respond with, 'Thank you for being open. I hear you want acknowledgment for your hard work and growth. But before we discuss that, have you thought about your next level of development? Where do you want to grow? Where do you see yourself in a year?'

You could also ask questions like:

- What is it that you've loved about this year?
- What area of the work has been most rewarding or most challenging?
- Where do you see that you've grown?
- Where would you like to grow?

You can contextualize these growth needs with what the company requires by starting a career conversation. You can then connect them to projects, programs, and people to help them develop.

Once you have addressed their growth needs, you might shift their focus from pay to a more holistic personal development conversation. 'A pay rise is not 100 percent within my control, but I'm going to record this conversation and communicate your growth potential as part of my team's remuneration review.'

I Deserve a Promotion

A typical career conversation is with those who desire to move into management. People often think they want to be a manager because they have more visibility and might get paid more.

Within most organizations, there are two tracks:

1. Subject matter expert—where you become better and better at what you do
2. Management—tends to be a bit more general and requires people skills.

Using BIRCH, you can uncover if doing the work engages them. Or maybe they are engaged in helping others achieve their goals. As you are discovering, to be an effective manager, you must focus on scaling yourself as well as your people. So, if they love doing the work they are trained in, then maybe the conversation helps them understand how they can grow in their area of specialty.

I Don't Know What I Want to Do

Another career conversation is with those who have been with the company for about five years, and when asked about growth desires, they have no idea. BIRCH can help you uncover whether this person is a solid performer who is happy in their role or a person who is not taking ownership of their career and is burning out.

In either case, growth is required to future-proof their contribution. As the maxim goes: 'Even if you are on the right road, if you are not moving forward, you will get run over.'

You might dig deeper by asking, 'You've got institutional knowledge that's really important to the company, so how can we get you to share that knowledge?' There are many ways of engaging these people by helping them feel like a valuable member of the team. I will share more ideas in the play on talents and coaching.

PRACTICE:

PREPARE AND SCHEDULE CAREER CONVERSATIONS WITH YOUR TEAM.

PLAY #8: DECISIVENESS

In any moment of decision, the best thing you can do is the right thing. The worst thing you can do is nothing.

—Theodore Roosevelt

Amazon, the world's largest online retailer and a prominent cloud services provider, has adopted leadership principles as a way of codifying its leadership framework. Of note is number nine: bias for action. The Amazon explanation for bias for action is that 'speed matters in business. Many decisions and actions are reversible and do not need extensive study. We value calculated risk-taking.' (Leadership principles, n.d.)

Bias for action is decisiveness, and the definition of decisive [dih-sahy-siv] is:

1. having the power or quality of deciding; putting an end to controversy
2. characterized by or displaying no or little hesitation; resolute, determined
3. indisputable; definite

The antithesis of decisiveness is inaction or procrastination. Lack of decisiveness results in multiple and prolonged meetings, delays, resource consumption, and missed opportunities.

The following story illustrates the importance of decisiveness in terms of economic and human costs.

In 2013, Gustavo was the general manager for an international baby formula company in Thailand. The supplier informed the company that there was possible contamination by a bacterium that causes botulism. Untreated, botulism can prove fatal in babies, so this was of serious concern.

Initially, the supplier issued batch numbers of the product with possible contamination so that only a partial recall would be necessary. Whilst Gustavo and his team met to discuss how to execute this, he had his secretary call his wife because he had a six-month-old baby at home who was taking the formula. His wife took a picture of the batch number on the box and sent it to Gustavo's phone. During the meeting, he looked at the image, and his heart sank; the number on the box was from the suspected batch. He told his wife to call an Uber and take their precious baby straight to the hospital.

Gustavo and his team could not be sure whether the contamination was limited to that batch, so they decided to make a costly and complicated total recall. Gustavo slept at the office for three nights as he and his team frantically arranged to get every single product off the shelves, whether from major retailers or from little mom-and-pop shops that were only accessible by motorbike.

The good news was the box that Gustavo's wife photographed had not yet been used with the baby, who had only consumed formula from a non-suspect batch and is a healthy nine-year-old today. He was able to get a message to her that all was well and to turn the Uber around and go home.

Through Gustavo and his team's decisiveness and having a bias for action, the brand did not suffer, and once it was realized that the whole thing was a false alarm, the company was back to full market position within nine months.

When Gustavo told me this story, I empathized with the anguish he must have experienced having to stay at his post, whilst his precious baby might be sick from a product from the very company he was working for. His decisiveness under duress was driven by being human, and whilst it cost the company in the short-term, it delivered long-term results. I hope you never face such a dilemma, but I hope this story sticks with you as a reminder that our decisions matter.

For several years, I have conducted a program on decisiveness for a Japanese bank.

Decisiveness is challenging for this bank, as Japanese culture values collaborative decision-making. The Japanese follow the principle of *nemawashi*, which is a term from gardening and means to uncover the roots. In business, *nemawashi* works by listening to each part of the organization and addressing needs through one-on-one discussions and small meetings.

Decisiveness and *nemawashi* can seem in conflict unless we understand ownership and responsibility. We can, and should, have a bias for action, be decisive in areas where we have full ownership and responsibility, and use *nemawashi*/collaboration when more stakeholders are involved or required to get the job done.

Lack of productivity and human cost occurs when people wait for decisions because they don't feel empowered to make them. By adopting the principle of bias for action, Amazon sends the message that it wants its leaders to take ownership and be decisive.

When a leader takes ownership, they can have a significant and evident impact on their environment and will be a driver or shaper of the company's culture. In contrast, those who are passive, just passengers, or worse, act like victims, will hinder progress.

A great role model for bias for action and empowering her team is Mel Dreuth, a chief people officer and a contributor to this book. When Kelsey joined Mel's team, she was told, 'If there is something you don't like, change it. You won't hurt my feelings. I'm empowering you. If you have questions, I'm here. Otherwise, just do it.'

For the first week, Kelsey took notes, saw areas for improvement, and started investigating solutions. A few days later, her manager shared thirty, sixty, and ninety-day goals with Kelsey. The goals were almost completely aligned with the work Kelsey was already doing. Kelsey knew the *why* and was empowered to make progress. This alignment of decisiveness with ownership is very motivating. Following this, Kelsey completely restructured the company's new hire process.

Decisive people shape their environment using language like 'I will' and 'you can', whereas people who lack decisiveness freeze in the face of uncertainty. This is understandable because the human brain likes certainty. Think about your brain as always trying to conserve energy. The brain does not want to take on too much processing, so it looks for shortcuts and ways to minimize the number of decisions required. The result is that, whilst shortcuts are comfortable, making an unfamiliar decision feels uncomfortable.

Using This Play

Encouraging your people to be more decisive starts with confidence, a play we have already covered. Next, you need to assess their tolerance for uncertainty and calibrate it for the context of the work you do.

Colonel Colin Powell, former leader of US forces in Operation Desert Storm and former Chairman of the Joint Chiefs of Staff, had a formula for dealing with uncertainty in decision-making. This formula encourages informed yet swift decision-making by setting a minimum and maximum threshold for the probability of success.

P= 40 to 70%
Where P is the probability of success

Figure 19: Decision Formula

Informed yet swift decision-making is the crux of this formula. It says a probability of success below forty percent is too risky, and you need to be more informed. But waiting for the probability to move above seventy percent may invalidate the opportunity through procrastination, and the action will be too late to make meaningful progress. So, procrastination in the name of reducing risk actually increases risk.

I find it interesting that the more senior leaders I coach usually have an uncertainty quotient around sixty-five percent, but middle managers prefer a certainty above eighty percent, which, as we see from the formula, is outside the sweet spot.

REFLECTION:

DO YOU THINK THAT PEOPLE GET TO SENIOR MANAGEMENT BECAUSE THEY ARE MORE DECISIVE, OR HAVE THEY BECOME MORE DECISIVE AS THEY HAVE ACHIEVED GREATER SENIORITY?

I have also observed that teams take their cue from their manager on how decisive to be.

In developing decisiveness with your team, you might want to share the model that works for your context. From the complex Yetton Vroom model to the simple ICED model that works well for most situations.

I IDENTIFY THE GAP

C CREATE A LIST OF POSSIBLE ACTIONS TO CLOSE THE GAP (CHECK FOR BIASES).

E EVALUATE THE EFFECTIVENESS OF THE ACTION

D DECIDE ON THE BEST ACTION TO CLOSE THE GAP.

ICED starts with identifying the gap, which could be a problem or an opportunity for improvement. Then, you create a list of possible actions to close the gap. These actions may require collaboration with others, so actions include getting buy-in. Next, evaluate the actions for effort, effectiveness, and risk. The best decision is likely to be the one that balances the least effort, the most effectiveness, and the lowest risk. Finally, decide on the actions you will take and execute them.

Don't forget that your decisions and actions can be adjusted as new information becomes available. So, it's important to monitor the impact your decisions and actions have so you can have a bias for action and make in-process changes to adjust for new information.

Over time, you will get more comfortable with uncertainty and make decisions with more confidence, speed, and certainty.

Cognitive bias plays a huge role in how we make decisions, so I have added a self-check at the second step of the ICED model. Psychologists have labels for over 180 types of cognitive bias, but they can be generalized into:

How we remember—memories are not facts. How we recall depends on how we emotionally coded the memory at the time of creation and what we added to or deleted from it over time.

Too much information—because we are overwhelmed with information, we tend to believe things that confirm our bias or notice things that are primed, repeated, or stand out as different.

Not enough meaning—we tend to add our own meaning to information, adding our own stereotypes or simplifying the complex to fit our worldview. Adding to this, the tendency to mind-read what other people are thinking creates a potent brew of intoxication.

The need to act fast—because of the urgency to get things done, we tend to focus on the information that is immediately in front of us and fail to step back and take a strategic perspective.

REFLECTION:

WHAT IS YOUR CURRENT LEVEL OF DECISIVENESS—COULD IT BE INCREASED?

TO WHAT EXTENT ARE YOU COMMUNICATING DECISIVENESS—COULD IT BE ENHANCED?

The agile approach stems from software development processes. Not so long ago, software developers would work months, or even years, on a new product update, which was released with a big bang. Think of the years between Microsoft Office versions in the 2000s or the quarters or years between Apple iTunes desktop software releases. Developers spent a lot of time building a ton of new features and then released them all at once.

Agility takes an iterative approach, which we see from most software developers today. It turns massive, cumbersome releases into small, fast, agile projects that minimize effort, potential bugs, incompatibilities, and impact to users. It delivers more new features to customers faster and with fewer errors, which shows continuous progress and improvement. This is why your web browser, mobile phone, and messaging app are frequently updated with new features or bug fixes. The changes are rarely ground-breaking; they are small, measurable improvements that happen often.

Leaders can learn from the agile approach by using incremental progress to reduce procrastination, thereby lowering risk and encouraging a bias for action. It's helpful to ask: 'What is the small action we can take with sufficient certainty it will move us towards our desired outcome?' This is a bias for action and a constant effort to move the ball forward.

PRACTICE:

WHERE CAN YOU DEMONSTRATE DECISIVENESS IN THE NEXT FEW DAYS?

ONCE IDENTIFIED, HAVE A BIAS FOR ACTION AND BE DECISIVE.

PLAY #9: TALENT + STRENGTHS

Talent is like electricity. We don't understand electricity. We use it.

—Maya Angelou

Imagine you are the coach of a sports team. You will want to acquire great players and play the ones you have in their best positions. In addition, you will be developing skills and maximizing the talent of your players.

The word talent is of Latin origin, meaning scale, balance, and sum. In ancient Greek and Roman times, it was one of several units of mass and a commercial weight.

Talent often refers to a company's entire workforce or candidates they are interested in hiring. Like a coach, your role as a leader is to hire and get the best from your talent.

To effectively hire and develop people, it is valuable to realize that true talent, the natural ability for exceptional performance, is rare. On the other hand, skill is acquired through training and hard work.

Strength is another term that is often misunderstood. A strength is a talent or skill applied in specific contexts to create exceptional and consistent performance. Strength is a function of capacity (talent plus skills), the opportunity to apply this capacity, and willingness to take action.

This forms a useful acronym—COW.

Strength = Capacity X Opportunity x Willingness

Figure 20: Strength Formula

I was coaching a pharmaceutical marketing executive from Vietnam on executive presence, and she asked my advice about a member of her team.

'He was doing fine in his previous role, but now that he has been promoted, he is missing deadlines, and I don't know what to do.'

People can have the capacity and willingness but not the opportunity to show them in their current role. Or, you might have employees with capacity and opportunity who do not show willingness. Or, you might have people with opportunity and willingness who lack the capacity. On examination, the member of the marketing team lacked capacity, and this diagnosis meant the next steps were obvious.

Before applying this formula to your team, I recommend applying it yourself. For this exercise, honestly consider the following four leadership strengths and your capacity, opportunity, and willingness with a low, medium, or high rating. The results will give you insights into where you will shine and where you might need some additional focus.

	CAPACITY	OPPORTUNITY	WILLINGNESS
STRATEGIC THINKING			
OPERATIONAL EXECUTION			
RELATIONSHIP BUILDING			
INFLUENCE			

Peter Drucker, the famous management guru, noted most managers are unaware of their own strengths. This exercise, together with a conversation with your manager or coach, will help overcome any potential weaknesses. This grid brings into perspective that we should not overdo our strengths or ignore our weaknesses. A good manager is a well-rounded manager.

'To the man with a hammer, everything looks like a nail.'

—Abraham Maslow

'Strengths get managers ahead. Weaknesses get them fired.'

—Marcus Buckingham

REFLECTION:

ARE YOU COLLABORATING WITH PEOPLE WHO HAVE COMPLEMENTARY STRENGTHS?

HAVE YOU BUILT A TEAM THAT MITIGATES YOUR WEAKNESSES?

ARE YOU BROADENING YOUR PERSPECTIVES BY LEARNING OUTSIDE YOUR AREA OF STRENGTH?

WHAT WILL YOUR AREA FOR SELF AND PROFESSIONAL DEVELOPMENT BE?

USING THIS PLAY

> Real humility is not hiding your own strengths;
> it's showing others the strength they possess.

The better you know yourself (self-leadership), the better you can lead others. Now that you have applied the COW acronym to yourself, consider each immediate team member and create a map of their potential based on their role. Not for the individuals but for their role. For example, some roles might give an opportunity to gain visibility, make a ground-breaking advancement, or improve the company's performance. Other roles might be supportive and have fewer opportunities but are critical to reaching goals.

	CAPACITY	OPPORTUNITY	WILLINGNESS
ROLE 1			
ROLE 2			
ROLE 3			

Now that you have determined the potential for each role's COW of strength, you can better measure each team members' performance against the potential of their role. You can do this alone or as part of a career conversation.

This exercise results in a nine-box grid (Figure 21), which can help you evaluate performance and potential and then develop a path forward. For example, if a role has a low potential, but an individual performs highly in that role, they would be a good candidate for further development in higher-potential roles. This map helps you see the potential of each member of your team rather than just their current performance.

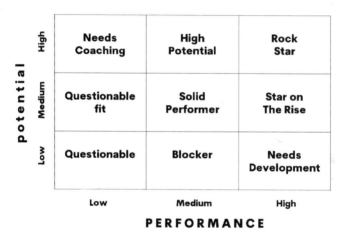

Figure 21: Nine-Box Grid

With a growth mindset, you can now develop your people. You will get the most improvement when you focus on developing their strengths. Don't expect people to turn their weaknesses into strengths on their own; it's not going to happen. Place or pair people with others who have complementary strengths and ensure their differences are appreciated, respected, and harnessed.

Developing people is an ongoing process of feedback and coaching. Everyone, including you, is a work in progress. Understanding this puts progress over perfection. We should all focus on being better today than yesterday and set goals to be better tomorrow.

Not everyone on your team will be a rock star, which is good. Solid performers still get great results when given the right opportunity.

To increase performance or mitigate non-performance, you will need to become an effective coach (Play #12) or have crucial conversations (Play #10). Developing talent is key to scaling any organization, and your ideal team member might be struggling in another department or vice versa.

PRACTICE:

USING THIS PLAY EFFECTIVELY IS OFTEN A COLLABORATION WITH THE PEOPLE AND CULTURE TEAM, DEDICATED HUMAN RESOURCE BUSINESS PARTNER, AND YOUR MANAGER. SCHEDULE A CALL TO TALK ABOUT MEMBERS OF YOUR TEAM.

PLAY #10 CRUCIAL CONVERSATIONS

Be brave enough to start a conversation that matters.

—Margaret Wheatley

What if you've explained the why, set clear objectives, and given FIF feedback, but a person on your team still doesn't demonstrate decisiveness and is unable to achieve results?

Using the nine-box grid from the Talent and Strengths play, if they are questionable or a questionable fit, you will need to have a crucial conversation.

There is a whole book on Crucial Conversations (Patterson & Grenny, 2011), which states that these conversations happen when:

- stakes are high
- opinions differ
- emotions run strong.

Given that the number one reason my students on leadership programs tell me for not speaking up is fear of hurting people's feelings, you will to need get your head in the game for this play.

The first mindset that you need to have is that the cost of not having the conversation is greater than having it. Allowing people to continue to non-perform frustrates you, irritates teammates, and likely erodes the self-confidence of the non-performer.

The People Mindset Model showed that we should not rescue or blame people but communicate potential (growth), challenge for improvement, and coach for change. The way to do this is to set a positive intention and:

Put the fish on the table

Putting the fish on the table is a metaphor for a frank and open conversation. If a fish is under the table and we don't know about it, it will rot and smell, but if we put the fish on the table, we can cook it and eat it. Putting the fish on the table is my name for a Crucial Conversation strategy that will make you a more effective people manager.

Your positive intention should be to be respectful to the individual and do the right thing for your team and the company. When you set this intention, you can be direct and empathetic, and not defensive.

Another mindset my clients have found useful is to separate office from officer. You have probably seen TV coverage of the president of the United States walking across the White House lawn and being saluted by a uniformed marine as he boards the presidential helicopter. That marine is saluting the office of the president, not the officer. At the time of writing, the officer holding that office is Joe Biden; his predecessor was Donald J Trump, and before that, Barack Obama. Each of these officers has their own strengths and weaknesses, but the office is what holds the power.

Being a CEO, or head of sales, in an office, and the holder of that office is an officer. When we have a Crucial Conversation, it helps if we speak as the office and not the officer. For example, 'As chief technology officer, I need to make decisions about security, and whilst I would love to grant your request, I must say no because of security issues.'

Using this Play

Office and officer is a useful frame when you need to have crucial conversations and put the fish on the table with colleagues. Follow these steps for more effective conversations:

1. Put the fish on the table.
2. Check your narrative and theirs.

3. Acknowledge their feeling/own yours.
4. State your needs.
5. Make a request and seek agreement.

Put the fish on the table

Calmly state the facts of the issue as you see them (no silence or blame). This is almost identical to the first F, Facts, in the FIF feedback model.

You will have gathered evidence from observation and be able to say: 'I am observing behavior X with result Y, and as previously discussed, this is not acceptable.'

Check your narrative and theirs

What are you telling yourself about this situation? What is their story?

It's valuable to share what you think about the situation and get their story. It might go something like this:

'I can't understand why this is happening. I have given you feedback and provided support, so I'm wondering if you can tell me what's going on?'

Acknowledge their feeling/own yours

The previous step is likely to flush out some emotional language, which you will need to acknowledge if you are to move forward.

'I'm sorry to hear you feel …'

'When I hear you talk about your reasons/feelings on this issue, I feel … (insert emotion such as disappointed, frustrated, confused, let down).'

State your needs

The reason for this conversation and your emotion is an unfulfilled need. Now is the time to state your needs in direct and unequivocal terms. This statement is a path forward, and the other party must either follow this path, or there is no future in the current position.

You might say something like: 'OK, I need you to understand that behavior X with results Y cannot continue, and you will need to change.'

Make a request and seek agreement

Once you have stated your need for change, unequivocally spell out or paint a picture of the path forward and get agreement. It might sound like this:

'So moving forward, you will do ... and achieve ... Do you agree?'

In my introduction, I mentioned that the challenge for managers is to have empathy whilst holding people accountable. The way to do that is to set clear expectations and give regular feedback. By hiring for talent and mindset whilst developing skills and creating a culture where people can thrive, you will minimize the need for crucial conversations.

Over my career as an executive coach and C-suite advisor, I have had many conversations with leaders struggling with a team member who is not performing. Usually, they have delayed having the crucial conversation, and it has come to the point where that employee needs to go.

Collins (2001) called it 'getting the right people on the bus'. This means getting people who are not performing off the team. When my clients finally decide and let the person go, they typically say the same thing: 'I wish I'd done that six months ago.'

Perhaps they should have had the crucial conversation three to six months before that.

My Fish on the Table framework draws from the concept of Nonviolent Communication (Rosenberg, 2003), which I connected to the ownership of emotions in my *Self Leadership* book (2012, pp 78-80). The message here is you must take responsibility for your role and hold the other person accountable for theirs. This will never be an enjoyable play, but it is a critical one. As previously mentioned, leadership is not a popularity contest, but you will sleep better at night if you make the right decisions and don't procrastinate.

PRACTICE:

IDENTIFY A CRUCIAL CONVERSATION YOU NEED TO HAVE. PLAN FOR IT AND HAVE IT.

PLAY #11: CULTURE

> *"Leadership is about the team - the culture they keep and embrace, it's about empathy for your customers, clients, employees and the communities where you do business, it's about doing the right thing for the right reasons, being confident enough to take risks and responsible enough to think of those who your decisions and risks may affect."*
>
> —Kat Cole

I spoke with Rebecca Clements, head of people and culture for several successful start-ups. Microsoft has just acquired her most recent company, and I asked her what she looks for when assessing culture.

> It starts with the CEO. Who are they? What's their style? How are they in good times? Are they the tough times? How do they motivate people? What do they value? What do they believe in? How do they show up? What kind of communicator are they? What kind of team that they assembled? Because that shows their belief in how important leadership is within the company. Right?

Culture starts from the top, and no matter how strong your strategic plan, its efficacy will be held back by members of your team if they aren't aligned with your culture. In other words:

> *Culture eats strategy for breakfast.*
>
> —Peter Drucker (2006)

Within a few moments of your mother bringing you into the world, you had a name, a nationality, an ethnicity, a gender, and possibly a religion and a football team to follow—you have been framed!

A frame determines how you experience and respond to the world. Just as the last thing a fish can discern is water, we are often oblivious to how culture influences our behavior. And, as we go to school, join a team, club, or gang, we are indoctrinated into new cultural norms that subtly control us. We dare not break these unwritten rules for fear of being ostracized, excommunicated, or voted off the island.

The above description may seem negative, but so far, we have survived as a species because of our ability to gather in tribes and for tribes to congregate in towns and then cities. Knowing how culture works allows you to create a culture within your team or organization that nurtures growth and allows people to thrive.

Operating at the cultural level is the key to transformational leadership (Burns, 1978) and (Bass, 1985). The followers of a transformational leader feel trust, admiration, loyalty, and respect for the leader and are willing to work harder than originally expected. These outcomes occur because the transformational leader offers followers something more than just working for self-gain; they give them an inspiring mission, vision, and identity.

Culture can be defined as the ideas, beliefs, customs, and social behaviors of a particular group. Culture can be expressed in a simple formula: X (behavior) equals Y (result) in C (culture).

C=Culture

X behavior = Y Result

Figure 22: Culture Formula

In some Asian countries and many Western organizations, the behavior (X) of speaking up before your boss would result in (Y) being labeled a troublemaker or disrespectful. In Japan, there is a culture of inviting junior team members to speak first, so they are not influenced by the HIPO, the highest-paid officer.

I encourage my C-level clients to learn from this Japanese practice because it creates a culture of diversity and inclusion. After all, nobody has a monopoly on a good idea.

In the new normal of multicultural teams working remotely and communicating by email, Slack, or Zoom, you have the opportunity to mold the culture that brings out the best in your people and allows you to scale the company.

Walk into any Google office, and you will see colorful beanbags and a fully stocked canteen with free food for staff. Many have tried to copy this, but getting rid of cubicles and creating co-working spaces may not be enough. People are certainly influenced by their environment, but they are more impacted by the behaviors of people they respect. If you are their leader, that means you, and so you must articulate the X=Y in everything you say or do.

Many organizations attempt to create a culture by a well-drafted value statement that they paid an external consulting company to create. Values are important. Values, like beliefs, guide us in how we behave in situations. A value helps us solve a dilemma where choices of behaviors could be equally right or wrong. Problems arise when leaders do not live the stated values or are inconsistent in applying them.

In the next section, I share specific leadership principles that guide each of the plays you have read here. Whilst by no means exhaustive, these principles can be a starter for you to think about what's important to you, your team, and your company.

Therefore, this playbook is a way of creating a culture or way of being. Each specific play helps you understand as a leader how to model, reinforce, and reward behaviors that align with your desired culture.

USING THIS PLAY

Once you have decided on the culture you wish to create or reinforce, you will want to be role modeling, reinforcing, and rewarding behaviors aligned with this culture. For example, if you state: 'We are a team that listens to each other', you had better get good at listening and demonstrating that you are listening.

It takes time and effort, but also empathy and compassion to truly model the behaviors that can best help those on your team. Reinforcement is a powerful leadership tool to encourage and recognize good behavior. Nearly all creatures respond well to praise and positive reinforcement, resulting in repetition of the behaviors that gained them praise.

Rewards provide additional value to desired behaviors. These can be opportunities for growth, a round of applause, or tangible rewards, such as celebrations, time off, or even a t-shirt or sticker. Monetary rewards, such as a goal-based bonus, can incentivize desired behaviors, but they are far from the only way.

We use and encourage these efforts because they work. Multiple studies (Lonczak, 2021) point to increases in performance when incentives, rewards, and reinforcement are put into practice.

You can be a culture creator by role modeling, reinforcing, and rewarding your team using what you've learned in this entire playbook.

Play #1: The Why	Always seek to know why you are doing anything and communicate the importance of each objective or key result.
Play #2: Ownership	Have a growth mindset to challenge yourself and your team to take ownership in each situation. Reward with public praise those who go above and beyond to take ownership. Hold yourself and your people accountable for actions and inaction.

Play #3: Feedback	Use feedback as a gift to provide insights using the FIF framework so your people can grow. Constantly reinforce that there is no failure, only feedback for improvement.
Play #4: Objectives	Always be clear about your objectives, and when communicating objectives, always confirm understanding. Reinforce behaviors that move the team closer to goals, and reward your team with celebrations when objectives are achieved.
Play #5: Confidence	Step into your own confidence using 3A and encourage your team to be confident in their abilities. Reinforce the idea that if you've done it, it's not bragging. Reward confident actions with a round of applause.
Play #6: Collaboration	Role model the free sharing of ideas and listen to the ideas of others. Reinforce zero tolerance for land grabs and turf wars. Reward initiatives that require sharing of ideas and resources for a common objective.
Play #7: Career Conversations	Regularly have conversations with your team about how they can progress their career. Reinforce that career development is a shared responsibility and reward those who take ownership of their careers with opportunities to grow and gain visibility.
Play #8: Decisiveness	Make decisions in the presence of uncertainty. Reinforce a bias for action by encouraging your team to do the same. Reward and recognize a bias for action by giving examples of people using this mindset to achieve objectives.

Play #9: Talent & Strengths	Treat people as individuals with talents and skills and look for opportunities for them to willingly apply these talents and skills. Reinforce that you value everyone's talents and skills and reward their willingness to apply them.
Play #10: Crucial Conversations	Address different perspectives early, in a respectful and supportive way. Reinforce that passive-aggressive behavior will not be tolerated, and reward those who can address conflict in constructive ways.
Play #11: Culture	Be a model of the company culture. Reinforce and reward behaviors that align with the culture and values. Explain that we do it this way is because of our culture.
Play #12: Coaching	Demonstrate you believe in your team's potential for growth and are committed to supporting the growth objectives that are important to them. Be a role-model coach by asking rather than telling.

Imagine a new employee, Ryan, with five years of experience at their previous employer and just a few months at your company. Their previous employer's culture was one of hierarchy and a strict rule to follow the chain of command. One day, Ryan has a problem with the work of a colleague in a different department. Because of Ryan's experience with his previous company's culture, he escalates this problem to you, his manager. Ryan expects you will talk to the colleague's manager, who would then reprimand or correct the behavior of the colleague.

Is this efficient? Is this aligned with your culture and this playbook?

PRACTICE:

1) PLAN HOW YOU WOULD RESPOND TO RYAN AND MODEL, REINFORCE, AND REWARD YOUR PREFERENCE FOR OWNERSHIP?

2) ADDRESS ANY OUTSTANDING CULTURAL ISSUES IN YOUR TEAM.

PLAY #12: COACHING

Coaching's not a job, it's a privilege.

—Lee Corso

Today's effective leader must be able to coach. Coaching helps a person move from point A (where they are) to point B (whom or where they want to be). This is the last, and probably the most important, of the plays. It is last because coaching is the culmination of the expectations, mindsets, and behaviors of all the other plays.

As a manager or leader, you spend a lot of time telling people what you would like them to do and why it is important. You may also be telling and showing people how to do things, but coaching is none of these. Coaching is asking, listening, and facilitating a greater understanding of what problems and opportunities a person is experiencing (the *outer* game) and how they think about it (the *inner* game). Coaching helps people make their own choices to behave in ways that move them towards a more effective version of themselves.

Good coaching encourages ownership and decisiveness, in short, self-leadership. Whilst it takes time to coach the people on your team, it pays dividends in increasing efficiency and agility. Therefore, developing and continuously improving coaching skills is a great professional development objective for every leader.

USING THIS PLAY

To be an effective coach, imagine stepping into a mental shower that washes away all your agendas, judgments, and pre-existing views and then fills you with curiosity for how you can support this person in reaching their objectives. This non-judgmental and unconditional positive regard for the person you are coaching is the secret ingredient for great coaches.

Prescription without diagnosis is malpractice.

I learned the above maxim during my training as a physiotherapist, and it is a powerful guide when coaching. In fact, good coaches do not prescribe at all; they help team members realize their best solution. This best solution is likely to align with the company's culture and vision. Otherwise, you coach the person to seek opportunities outside of their current employment.

Coaching requires both support and challenge. Support is demonstrated by open body language, a warm tone, and non-judgmental listening. Challenge is created by asking questions that confront a person's narrative about their reality, open up new choices and behaviors, and hold them accountable for those behaviors.

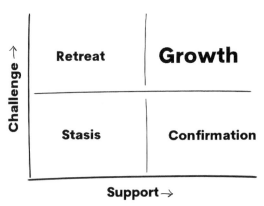

Figure 23: Coaching Challenge and Support

REFLECTION:

ARE YOU, BY DEFAULT, BETTER AT SUPPORT OR CHALLENGE?
ANSWERING THIS QUESTION HONESTLY SHOWS WHAT YOU
NEED TO WORK ON TO BE A MORE EFFECTIVE COACH.

With a growth mindset, we do not rescue or blame; we grow people by communicating their potential, challenging them for improvement, and coaching them for change.

As a mental exercise, think about a problem or opportunity that someone on your team is currently facing. Now step back from this situation and realize that it has two parts, which coaches call the inner game and the outer game, from the book, The Inner Game of Tennis (Galway, 1997). See Figure 24.

Problem or opportunity

INNER GAME
The mental map about the situation, including biases, beliefs, values, meanings, metaphors, and more.

OUTER GAME
The reality of the situation, including facts, people, measurements, observations, criteria, and more.

Figure 24: Inner and Outer Game

Let's now try to coach someone through this situation. You start indexing the outer game by gently asking probing questions about who, what, where, and when.

We explored these questions when we looked at behaviors in the leadership operating system. When asked with gentle curiosity, these questions help people see how they have created a story about the situation. Is it an opportunity or a crisis? Have they explored all the options? Or have they taken things personally, generalized or catastrophized the situation, and painted themselves into a corner?

Using questions to shine a light on a person's representation of reality helps put them in the driver's seat (ownership) and see options.

Once we have probed the outer game, we can ask inner game questions to understand how the person thinks and feels about the situation. What's their inner narrative, their values, beliefs, and meanings? Exploring the inner game opens the possibility to reframe the situation and choose new behaviors.

> The problem itself isn't as important as how
> the person has framed the problem.

Inner Game questions:

These questions can help you build relationships and get a deeper understanding of a person.

You could simply ask, 'What kind of X is that X?' where X is the problem or opportunity. This kind of question causes the person to find a metaphor or share their narrative. When they share, you follow up with: 'Is there anything more about X?'

With this approach, you will often find that a person reframes themselves and sees more options.

A more probing approach would be to ask the following types of questions:

- What's important to you about X?
- What does X mean?
- What do you believe about X?
- What are you assuming about X?

As you ask these questions, X morphs with each question. So your next question uses the latest version of X that they shared with you.

Here's an example conversation between a manager and Harper, a team member the manager is coaching. Harper is overwhelmed by customer feedback on a recent software release (point A). She wants to move from feeling overwhelmed to regaining control (point B).

The manager asks, 'What's happening, specifically?'

Harper replies, 'Well, our customers say the new release is rubbish, and I'm worried they won't renew their license.'

The manager could ask Harper for specification about how she has made this situation personal, about her judgment of 'rubbish' (what was the actual issue?), or the pervasive nature of pointing to multiple customers. The manager chooses to go with customers first.

'Are all of our customers upset, or just some specifically?'

'Well, actually, it's mostly ABC Inc, but they are a major customer.'

'Yes, ABC Inc is a major customer. I wonder why they think this release is rubbish when other customers didn't?'

'Ah, well, it's probably because they have some custom modules we created for them, and the update team didn't know these.'

The outer game has been narrowed down from overwhelming to a specific customer and issue. The manager could have drillled further, but chose to be curious about Harper's inner game.

'So, you are telling me you are feeling overwhelmed that customer ABC is giving you negative feedback about the recent release. What does this mean to you?'

'Well, I need to keep customers happy all the time.'

This is a global narrative, and the manager could ask precision questions to challenge if this is even possible. Instead, they stayed with the inner game questions.

'What's important to you about keeping customers happy all the time?'

Anytime we ask an inner game question like 'What's important about ...' we get a person's values, beliefs, or identity. We get insight into their inner game, their 'mental map', and like any map, it is only accurate up to a point.

Harper might answer with something like, 'Well, it's important to be customer-centric, right?'

Answering a question with a question signals that Harper is looking for confirmation. It's possible it's not what she really believes. The manager continues to probe to ensure Harper takes ownership of the answer.

'Yes, being customer-centric is important, but what's really important to you?'

'It's important I do a good job.'

The manager could continue to pursue this framing of the issue, but it's good enough to challenge Harper using the original problem of feeling overwhelmed.

'So, you want to be customer-centric and do a good job, but you are becoming overwhelmed by one customer and one release. Is this the best way to look at this situation?'

'Oh ...'

Harper's inner game has revealed a mental map that is now open for some edits in the form of reframing.

Understanding How Frames Drive Behavior

In the above example, we asked Harper, 'What's important about ...', which gets the value frame for their mental map. As you can see from Figure 25, inner game frames drive communication and behavior.

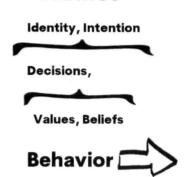

Coaching Questions

What are the beliefs, values, understandings that drive this behavior?

Inner Game Frames

Identity, Intention

Decisions,

Values, Beliefs

Behavior

Figure 25: Frames to Behavior

Reframing helps a team member find a new frame (narrative) to behave more effectively and efficiently. In the example, the frame is customer-centricity and doing a good job, but Harper won't achieve these in a sustainable fashion by being overwhelmed. So, the coaching continued as follows:

'The purpose of new releases is to improve features and benefits for customers, right?'

'Yes.'

'And in an ideal world, all releases would be bug-free, and all customers would praise you and the company, correct?'

'Yes.'

'Most of our customers were unaffected by the last update. And the customer that was affected was one that we had gone the extra mile to please in the past. So, to do a good job, you need to fix the exception and ensure it doesn't happen in the future, correct?'

'Yes.'

'So, what perspective will help you to handle this?'

'I need to stop panicking, start resolving the issue, and continue to communicate to the customer that we know the root cause. The issue was because of their custom settings, and we will be aware of this in the future to mitigate any problems.'

'Good! How do you feel now?'

'More in control.'

This is point B!

Start Stop Continue

The success of coaching is measured by a new mindset (frame) and new behaviors that deliver accelerated results. The behaviors will be in the form of something to start doing, stop doing, or continue doing.

Start: How can someone think creatively about the task at hand and provide a better solution? Activities may include improving processes or positively impacting the way the team operates.

Stop: What isn't working and is simply a waste of time, energy, and resources? One can stop activities that are ineffective, waste time or resources, or have a negative impact on the way people feel or the way things work. Activities may be technical or behavioral things that should cease.

Continue: Reflect on what's going well and how they do more of it. Review things the team has tried and were successful at but are not yet part of common practice. Once the activities are part of the way things are done, add them to processes and how the team works.

Start, stop, and continue is how you hold people accountable. Ending each coaching session by asking, 'What will you now start, what will you now stop, and what will you now continue?' frames the person for behavior. You have set clear expectations of what behaviors you will observe, and as your coachee has said these things, they have taken ownership.

At the beginning of this book, I said that the biggest challenges as a manager or leader in the new normal are showing empathy and holding people accountable; coaching is the way to do this.

This play, and all others, will help you become the best leader you can be. But to be a good leader, you must also know how to follow. To coach others, you must be coachable. Who is your coach?

> **PRACTICE:**
>
> PERHAPS YOU WOULD LIKE TO START COACHING YOUR TEAM MEMBERS TODAY. STOP TALKING WHEN YOU COULD ASK A QUESTION AND CONTINUE DEVELOPING TO BECOME YOUR BEST LEADER!

PART 4: LEADERSHIP PRINCIPLES

There are three constants in life ... change, choice and principles.

—Stephen Covey

Principles and rules both govern behavior. Rules or traditions are imposed from the outside and must be complied with, or you will face the consequences because they have been agreed upon by the community. Principles come from the inside. They are the fundamental ideas that answer the question, 'What is the right behavior?'

Andrew Glass is a trader. When I met Andrew, he was working with Anglo Americans and trading commodities such as iron, copper, and tin. I was curious how he remained unemotional when large amounts of money were at stake. When I asked him about this in an online summit in 2019, he responded:

A trader is looking at the opportunities that are in the market. I particularly focus on commodity markets, you can trade obviously, FX or any kind of commodity or financial instrument. And a trader is trying to look into the future to see what there's going to be worth in the future. So, you're doing your analysis and building a hypothesis. And you're trying to anticipate and take a position on where you think the markets are going to go in your specific area of expertise.

The idea of trading is that something will be worth more, to someone else, at the time you want to sell it.

So, you're very much going to have the humility to understand that no matter how good a trader you are, you can make mistakes and that the market again is bigger than what you are.

As previously mentioned, a principle is a fundamental truth or proposition that serves as the foundation for a system of belief or behavior or chain of reasoning. In this section, we are going to look at the principles that frame and inform your behavior with your people—the plays.

The principle that the market is bigger than he is and that he can make mistakes drives Andrew's behavior. He continued:

As a trader, we were playing; we're playing devil's advocate all the time. If I have an idea about a position that I want to step into and step into in size, and my conviction level is very good, I want someone to challenge me. Robust challenging is extremely important. You want people around you that also think and are going to push and test you and challenge you on your idea. And I might come from an eighty percent conviction down to a sixty or even a fourteen to Oh, that's the wrong direction! Okay, they've punched holes in my argument.

Andrew's behaviors of looking into the future, analyzing an opportunity using critical thinking, and then having people challenge him are what make him successful. Here, Andrew is using the leadership principle of Decisiveness. As an executive coach and c-suite advisor, I encourage leaders to do the same. Just as if they are playing chess and thinking, *If I move this, then they will move this …*

Good organizations publish their leadership principles to avoid ambiguity or confusion about what is expected of employees and leaders. Better organizations go further by adding clear definitions and having executives constantly reinforce those principles, both by their example and by their words.

For this book, I have selected a list of seven leadership principles. Is this an exhaustive list? Of course not, and I encourage you, as a leader, to reflect on the principles that drive your behaviors, and maybe you could add an eighth, ninth, or a tenth?

Leadership Principles

1. Self-leadership comes First

2. Leaders are Learners

3. Progress over Perfection

4. Disagree and Commit

5. Executive Presence

6. Build the Team

7. Diversity Matters

Figure 26: Leadership Principles

Self-leadership Comes First

You can't lead others unless you first lead yourself.

In 2017, it was my pleasure to interview the legendary Brian Tracy on self-leadership—a topic I have been speaking and writing about since 1999.

In case you don't know, Brian Tracy is a motivational speaker and self-development author of over seventy books. His popular titles include *Earn What You're Really Worth*, *Eat That Frog!* and *The Psychology of Achievement*.

You can watch my interview with Brian Tracy as part of the online resources. Here is part of what he said:

> Self-leadership is the starting point of everything. Self-leadership means that you decide exactly who you are and what you want, and then you write it down, and you make a plan and a goal, and you work on it every day. And especially Self-leadership means you accept complete responsibility for your results and outcomes; you don't blame other people, you don't make excuses, you say, 'I am responsible, I'm in control, I'm in charge of my own life'.
>
> And when you do that, it's the greatest source of personal empowerment that is possible as a human being. And every successful authority, over the decades, has realized that that is the starting point of everything. Without Self-leadership, nothing happens, and with Self-leadership, everything becomes possible.

This is an amazingly succinct and powerful explanation of self-leadership. In our book (Bryant & Kazan, 2012), Dr Ana Kazan and

I described it as: 'The practice of intentionally influencing your thinking, feeling, and actions towards your objectives.'

At the heart of your leadership is you. Therefore, you must first influence and lead yourself before influencing and leading others.

In 2010, a shy Spanish-speaking South American woman left her home and family to start a challenging new job in Singapore.

I asked her what she was thinking and feeling at that time. 'I was very afraid,' she said. 'But I thought I would be good because I was invited to be part of a big project.'

Then what was she afraid of? 'Of meeting people better than me,' she said.

I asked Valeria what she thought she brought to the job.; what strengths she had that would enable her to be good.

'I am very focused and understand the complexity of projects. I can work with different people from different cultures and build trust.'

I asked her, 'How many people in the world can do what you do, the way you do it?'

And her answer was, 'Not very many.'

So, I asked why she should be afraid that others would be better than her.

'I'm shy, and sometimes I have an idea, but I can't speak up in meetings.'

Valeria needed to learn to lead herself. She needed the self-awareness of her strengths, the self-regulation to project confidence, and the self-learning to adapt to a new culture.

Through our coaching together, Valeria realized that she is someone of value, that she has been through so many challenges and overcome them. She became aware that she had been negatively comparing herself with other people, and not only was this not helpful, but often the reverse was true. Valeria has stopped comparing and has been very successful as a leader on some complex projects.

Management guru and author Peter Drucker said: 'Being a self-leader is to serve as chief, captain, president, or CEO of one's own life.'

And Chinese Philosopher Lau Tsu said: 'Mastering others is strength; mastering oneself is true power.'

In times of crisis and ambiguity, self-leadership is particularly important. The leader must have self-awareness of their intentions and leadership style as well as self-management of their emotions and behaviors. This can be tough when the leader is facing uncertainty.

A self-leader sees options and grasps opportunities when others are waiting to be rescued.

An option is the power or liberty to choose. Often, we don't see our choices because of our framing or conditioning. Certainly, circumstances can restrict our liberty to choose, yet we always have a choice.

Viktor Frankl, author of *Man's Search for Meaning* (Frankl, 1946), and Jewish prisoner destined for the gas chamber in the Nazi death camps realized:

> Everything can be taken from a man but one thing: the last of the human freedoms—to choose one's attitude in any given set of circumstances, to choose one's own way.

This power to choose one's own intentions and actions is at the core of self-leadership. It is summed up in the poem *Invictus* (Henley, 1888) that inspired another prisoner, Nelson Mandela.

It matters not how straight the gate,

how charged with punishments the scroll,

I am the master of my fate:

I am the captain of my soul.

Do you know the meaning of the word opportunity? It means a favorable wind and comes from the Latin phrase *'ob portum veniens'* —coming toward a port.

During the height of the pandemic, I was coaching a CEO struggling with limited options to grow his company. We explored the metaphor of a sailing ship's captain when stuck in the doldrums (an area of little or no wind around the equator).

A good captain will set his crew to clean the boat and fix the sails, so when the wind returns, everyone and everything is ready to maximize the opportunity.

My CEO client took this metaphor and ensured his company was shipshape, so he could hoist the sails when opportunities returned. The result was two record-breaking quarters!

So, are you constantly considering your options? Are you ready to hoist your sails and take the opportunities when they arise?

I tell my coaching management students that to be a good leader, they need to buy a mirror as it is an essential management tool. Whenever your team is not performing, check the mirror, and ask yourself, 'Did I correctly set expectations?' Because you can't lead others unless you first lead yourself.

Other than a mirror, another way to check how you are doing is through a psychometric test. With help from Dr Paul Englert, I have developed the world's first Situational Judgment Test (SJT) for self-leadership, which I use with my clients.

SJTs capture a test taker's contextualized responses to examples of job situations. Participants are provided with video scenarios portraying situations they might face at work. Following each scenario is a series of items that represent how a person could respond. Participants are asked to evaluate these potential responses and arrange each one based on what they would most and least prefer to do. Their responses are used to make predictions about their future performance.

The SJT measures the three-core competencies—self-awareness, self-learning, and self-regulation.

Self-awareness is the tendency for an individual to focus and reflect on their own psychological processes, inner experiences, and their relationships with others.

Self-learning is the process by which individuals take the initiative in diagnosing their learning needs, goals, resources, and outcomes.

Self-regulation is the process of modulating attention, emotion, and behavior to a given situation/stimulus, for the purpose of pursuing a goal.

Take this psychometric and download a PDF of my 2016 book, *Self Leadership: 12 Powerful Mindsets & Methods to Win in Life and Business* (Bryant, 2016) from the online gateway.

Research on Future of Work Skill (Mckinsey, 2021) found employment was strongly associated with proficiency in several deltas within the self-leadership category, namely: adaptability, coping with uncertainty, synthesizing messages, and achievement orientation.

Self-leadership informs all the plays but especially Ownership and Confidence. Play #12: Coaching is all about getting people to operate with self-leadership.

> **CHALLENGE:**
> **TAKE SOME TIME TO IMAGINE THE BEST VERSION OF YOU. NOW, PUT ASIDE SOME TIME EACH DAY OR WEEK TO BECOME AWARE OF HOW YOU ARE MOVING TOWARDS YOUR IDEAL SELF.**

LEADERS ARE LEARNERS

Leadership and learning are indispensable to each other.

—US President John F. Kennedy

Many books about leadership contain long lists of leadership traits. I think such lists and memes are intimidating and not useful. Leaders, like you and me, are just people; we take risks and make mistakes. In my experience, what makes the difference is that leaders are learners; they learn from their mistakes and those of others and, therefore, get better.

It is important to realize that waiting to be perfect to lead or do anything is self-defeating—self-leadership involves taking action towards an objective. Leaders who operate this way notice and respond to actions that take them and their followers closer to the objective. In short, leaders are learners.

I was working with Darrel Metzger when he was the CEO of Sentosa Leisure Group in Singapore. I remember Darrel giving a speech to the staff of this service-driven organization. 'Make mistakes,' he said. 'Just don't make your mistakes bigger than mine.' He then explained how he made a million-dollar mistake during his time at Hong Kong Yacht Club.

By articulating his vulnerability, Darrel showed that leaders aren't perfect, and we should value progress instead. This made Darrel a very popular leader. I remember the day he was packing his office to move to a new role; people were crying in the corridors because they were sad to see him go.

Under Darrel's leadership, Sentosa Cove, a spectacular premium real estate development, and Resorts World, an integrated resort, were planned and built.

This principle informs the plays of The Why, Ownership, and Feedback.

Figure 27 shows how a leader acts in alignment with the intention (The Why), receives feedback, and owns their behavior to make the necessary adjustments.

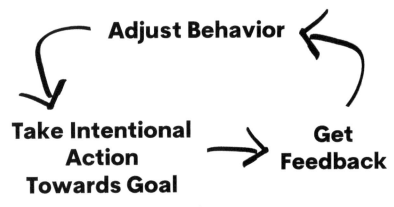

Figure 27: Leaders are Learners

> **CHALLENGE:**
>
> **WHAT ARE YOU CURRENTLY LEARNING, AND WHAT SHOULD YOU BE LEARNING?**

PROGRESS OVER PERFECTION

It is far more important to make continuous progress on projects and get things done than it is to guard against the possibility that mistakes will be made. But we don't boil the ocean. We break things down into smaller components that bring incremental value to the business.

—*Grant Halloran, CEO Planful Inc*

'Perfection is the enemy of progress' is a famous quote by Winston Churchill, but famous philosophers and writers throughout history have recognized this leadership principle. Voltaire, the French enlightenment writer, said: 'The best is the enemy of the good', and 'Better a diamond with a flaw than a pebble without' is attributed to Confucius.

A recent example of this principle in action can be found on the beautiful island of Mauritius. The Rogers Group, a diversified and services-based multinational operating in hospitality, property, logistics, and fintech, has its headquarters there. I am fortunate to have visited many times to work with the Rogers executive leadership team and have stayed at some of their beautiful resorts. The group's CEO, Philippe Espitalier-Noël, had the vision to transform the Bel Ombre region (a zone spanning some 4,300 hectares) from a sugar-cane-dependent area into a circular economy and sustainable living model for the world.

The project involved a collaboration between two of the group's divisions, Agria, the agriculture business, and their hospitality business. The sustainable living model presented new opportunities for the local community to thrive, the environment to be protected, and visitors to have unique experiences. There are golf courses for those who like to hit a small, elusive white ball, there's a beach club, a nature reserve, and the food comes 'farm to fork' from a short supply chain invigorating the local economy.

As the pandemic hit, borders closed and tourism came to a standstill globally. Rogers decided to practice progress over perfection by intentionally launching the Bel Ombre territorial brand, even though they couldn't shoot beautiful videos showing guests enjoying the facility. Rogers could have waited for the end of the pandemic to launch but chose to keep moving the needle.

Manish Bundhun, the chief people and transformational executive at Rogers, explained that the human effect of the decision to keep progressing was to motivate and engage the employees and give hope to the community that hospitality was not dead and would return. At the time of writing, the borders have reopened, and Bel Ombre is ready to receive visitors.

In my experience, a desire for perfection can be paralyzing. Why is this?

There can be many reasons, but fear of criticism is right up there. Overcoming this paralysis can be achieved by breaking down tasks into manageable pieces and showing how each piece adds value to the larger vision.

This principle only becomes part of company culture when leaders role model it by sharing their learning journey and validating progress rather than focusing on mistakes.

> **CHALLENGE:**
> **WHAT PROGRESS ARE YOU CURRENTLY MAKING THAT, WHILST NOT PERFECT, IS MOVING THE NEEDLE IN THE RIGHT DIRECTION?**

DISAGREE AND COMMIT

When we speak, we are afraid our words will not be heard or welcomed. But when we are silent, we are still afraid. So, it is better to speak.

—Audrey Lourde

Disagree and commit is a management principle pioneered by Andy Grove at Intel that states individuals are allowed to disagree whilst a decision is being made, but once a decision has been made, everybody must commit to it. It is a method of avoiding the consensus trap, in which the lack of consensus leads to inaction.

Companies other than Intel, such as Amazon, Sun Microsystems, and Qatar Airways have adopted this principle. Leaders who follow this principle are obligated to respectfully challenge decisions early in the decision-making progress when they disagree, even if doing so is uncomfortable or exhausting.

In my experience, this principle is one of the toughest to live. Why? Because to disagree when there is a large power differential could be a career-limiting move, and to disagree, you need a healthy relationship with conflict.

A few years ago, I worked with a Texas-based computer hardware company that had a plant in Malaysia and an office in Singapore. One of the company's leadership principles was Speak Up, but not surprisingly, this was not happening. Forgive me for stereotyping, but the more the extroverted and direct Texans encouraged their reserved, introverted, and collective-culture Asian colleagues to speak up—the quieter they became.

The cost of this silence was that creative insights were not shared in meetings, and possible problems were not flagged, resulting in a loss of productivity and competitive advantage. The cost to the individuals was that they were not considered leadership material, and their careers stagnated.

I ran a survey with the managers, which I have repeated with other groups, and the following list is the top ten reasons why people don't speak up:

1. We don't want to hurt their feelings.
2. They will misinterpret what we say.
3. They won't be receptive.
4. It will put our friendship at risk.
5. We will be open to retaliation or counterattack.
6. There's nothing in it for us.
7. It could backfire, and the problem could get worse.
8. It could escalate, and we don't like conflict.
9. We'll be out on a limb and won't be supported.
10. Nothing will change anyway.

Whether this cost is real or imagined, the mindset that speaking up is risky is prevalent.

Patrick Lencioni, in his book *The Five Dysfunctions of a Team* (Lencioni, 2002), notes that we need trust before we can have healthy conflict. Google's *Project Aristotle* research shows that psychological safety was the most important factor in high-performance teams, and the Radical Candor approach recognizes that we must demonstrate support before we can challenge.

When we need to speak up or disagree, we must frame our perspectives, being careful to avoid threatening people's worldviews.

Because if there is an opportunity for someone to take your communication as a personal attack, they probably will.

The challenge for the computer hardware company was Asia's strong frame of hierarchy: 'I won't speak up if there is somebody more senior than me in the room', and the concept of face: 'I will lose face if my idea is rejected or criticized.'

I helped the company set a frame that there are no bad ideas, and good ideas are independent of position in the company. This frame was set at the beginning of ideation meetings, and all participants were encouraged to be open and supportive.

You can set a frame by starting your communication with: 'In terms of … X' where X is a shared value for the parties. Frames help people contextualize the issue and not take things personally.

Consider these three frames about speaking up:

1. Speaking up is not costly; it is cost-saving.
2. Conflict is not bad; it is good to hear different perspectives.
3. Communication is not what we say, it is what others hear. Frame your communication for understanding.

CHALLENGE:

THERE IS LIKELY A PROCESS IN YOUR ORGANIZATION THAT YOU DISAGREE WITH. ARE YOU WILLING TO DISAGREE WITH IT AND, IF UNSUCCESSFUL, FULLY COMMIT TO THAT PROCESS?

EXECUTIVE PRESENCE

Executive Presence is credibility that goes beyond a title.

—Tom Henschel

The measure of leadership is influence, and to influence, you must have presence. We know that the Greek philosopher, Aristotle

(384–322 BC), understood this from his writings on rhetoric, the art of influence, and persuasion. Aristotle noted that influence occurs from the character of the speaker (*ethos*), the emotional state of the listener (*pathos*), or the argument (*logos*).

Whilst competence is important, it will not be enough to get you to the top of an organization and become the best leader you can be. You will need to develop your ethos, pathos, and logos. You will need executive presence.

> Executive presence is the ability to project gravitas, confidence, and poise under pressure, and to read the audience.

Gravitas, from Latin, means weight, dignity, and importance and conveys a sense of responsibility and commitment to the task.

Confidence in your abilities is a key success factor for anyone, yet so many people lack confidence. I believe confidence is not walking into a room thinking you are better than anyone else; that would be arrogance. It is walking into a room knowing you are the best version of yourself. You can achieve this by working on your self-leadership and realizing that leaders are learners.

Poise under pressure is a make-or-break quality for leaders. The ability to remain calm, rather than reactive, in stressful situations makes you stand out and influence. The secret is to breathe. Mentally, take a step back from the situation, assess your options, and look for opportunities. When you do this, you can have a bias for action and be decisive.

Reading the room requires empathy, which comes from the Greek word *pathos*. 'People don't care how much you know until they know how much you care' is a common quote attributed to many people, but it is a principle that holds true. In my mind, the key reason that executive presence is different from arrogance is that presence cares about what's important to others and how they feel. We explore this in the principles of collaboration and diversity matters.

Jeff Bezos said that personal brand is what they say about you after you leave the room, but I say executive presence will get you into the room in the first place.

Perhaps you can manage your employees because of your position and title, but you will need executive presence to collaborate with your peers and influence your boss and other stakeholders.

When leading smart people, managers need to remember Henry Ford, who said: 'The generalist will always employ the specialist.' The manager doesn't need to know everything about everyone's discipline. They need to know how to engage smart people to get the job done. Highly specialized people often miss the big picture and don't connect outside of their discipline. A good leader knows a bit about many different things and can use the best skills or combination of skills within the team to get the job done.

Confidence to influence laterally—to peers—comes from believing that your ideas are solid and knowing how to communicate the benefits of these ideas because you have empathized with what they are thinking and feeling. In an age of social networking, we should feel confident to socialize our ideas; after all, it is not the best ideas that get adopted but the best-supported ideas!

The executive presence to influence or manage upwards requires you to perceive your boss as an ally or team member. I don't mean to do away with respect or be over-familiar; however, realize that you are both accountable to the vision of the business/company. Like influencing laterally, ideas framed as beneficial to the business will be well received.

I once coached a senior manager who had a history of antagonizing clients and colleagues by telling them what he knew was the right thing to do. We discussed this, and he committed to stop telling and start empathizing and finding out how other people feel and what's important to them.

This change in behavior resulted in dramatic improvements in his relationships and efficiency. The efficiency result surprised him because he thought it would take longer to ask questions than to tell people what seemed an obvious solution.

If you are working in an international or global organization, your executive presence will need to be felt beyond your home base; you will need to be visible.

For example, a senior manager in India or Indonesia could be successfully managing thousands of people and meeting targets but have no visibility in a global organization. On the flip side, an American or European manager may fail to lead in Asia or South America because they don't understand how to get things done in those cultures.

A few years ago, I had a conversation with a US-based, but of Indian origin, C-level executive of a global company, about his managers from Asia. He expressed his frustration that in their own country, these leaders were failing to meet his criteria for leadership on a global stage. His leadership criteria could be summarized as follows. Leaders should:

- know their client's needs and wants
- have peer-level conversations with clients
- push back on clients or colleagues when there is a better way
- present convincingly to different demographics

- be comfortable to pick up the phone and challenge him or other senior stakeholders.

In short, executive presence.

One of my coaching clients, Dr Lakshmi, asked me whether she should take an MBA to improve her confidence to be influencial at work. As an external faculty member on MBA programs, I know they contain a lot of information and insights, but I doubted that it would help in this situation.

Lakshmi has a PhD in microbiology; she has written a best-selling cookery book, she has won a beauty contest, and is the mother of two boys. She didn't lack confidence; she lacked the ability to project her gravitas and confidence and to read the room. Lakshmi enrolled in my online executive presence program, and the transformation was tangible. She realized her value, stopped the self-defeating inner narrative, and learned to influence.

The results were immediate. She approached the senior leadership at her institution and highlighted a lack of support for women in Science, Technology, Engineering, and Mathematics (STEM). She asked for funding to run a program, which was promptly forthcoming, and she led that program as a keynote speaker.

Dr Lakshmi continues her science work, having received a promotion, and talks at conferences about the importance of women speaking up.

CHALLENGE:

WHERE DO YOU NEED TO SHOW UP WITH EXECUTIVE PRESENCE?

If you are interested in my online executive presence program, here's a link:

BUILD THE TEAM

> *Talent wins games, but teamwork and intelligence win championships.*
>
> —Michael Jordan

Nigel is sitting in his manager's office for his annual performance review. It had been a tough year; the effects of the COVID-19 pandemic had decimated his plans for the first two quarters, but Nigel had put in a superhuman effort and hit his targets in the third quarter. Nigel was expecting nothing but praise for his efforts, so imagine his surprise when his manager says, 'You have met your third quarter quota, Nigel, but I have some concerns about how you got there.'

All Nigel heard was 'I have some concerns'.

As we have discussed previously, the word 'but' has the effect of negating everything that precedes it. Being human is a paradox;

we are wired to be successful and competitive, but we can't do it alone.

What if we could eat our cake and have it too?

It sounds impossible, and with 'but' it is, so let me tell you a story.

An anthropologist was studying African tribes. He hung a bowl of fruit and candy on a tree branch and gathered the village children to him. 'We are going to have a race,' he announced. 'Whoever gets to the tree first wins the fruit and candy. Ready, set, go!'

On 'Go', the children held hands, walked to the tree, took down the bowl, sat in a circle, and shared the candy.

The anthropologist was confused by this behavior and asked the children why they behaved this way. They replied, '*Ubuntu*. How can one of us be happy if the others are sad?'

Ubuntu comes from the Zulu phrase '*Umuntu ngumuntu ngabantu*', which translates to 'a person can only be a person through others'. According to South African Archbishop Desmond Tutu, *Ubuntu* is the essence of being human.

Being human means being an individual AND part of a tribe (team). Legendary basketball coach Doc Rivers, who led the 2008 Celtics to their first NBA championship in twenty-two years, used the concept of *ubuntu* to bring individuals together as a team to achieve the win. In 2008, the Celtics had traded for three superstar players—Paul Pierce, Ray Allen, and Kevin Garnett, each of them was a leader in their own right. Coach Rivers told these superstars, 'You're going to have to change; it's not about who is best, it's about being best and about the team.'

Under Rivers' leadership, the *ubuntu* concept unified the Celtics. In practice, *ubuntu* means: 'I can't be all I can be unless you are all you can be. I can never be threatened by you because you're good because the better you are, the better I am.' It is the perfect concept for a team—turning a group of talented yet disparate individuals into a single, tight-knit unit.

Back to Nigel and his performance review. 'You have met your third quarter quota, Nigel, but I have some concerns about how you got there.'

Nigel's manager went on to explain. 'Nigel, you have made this quarter all about you. You have heroically visited every client and been part of every deal, but is this sustainable? Nigel, you have a team, and you are part of a team. Yes, your role is to meet the numbers, develop your people, and work with other parts of the business. Nigel, your attrition is the highest of any manager; your colleagues find you rude and demanding and they tell me you have refused their help when offered. Nigel, you look exhausted, and your people are demoralized. Is that the legacy you want to be remembered for?'

'But,' stammered Nigel, 'I thought you wanted the numbers?'

'I did, and I do,' said his manager. 'And it is possible to hit the numbers, coach your people, and collaborate with your peers if you take on the mindset of a leader, rather than try and be the hero.'

Whilst I am not an NBA coach, I have been an Executive Coach to leaders for nearly twenty-five years, and I can tell you that I have met many 'Nigels'. So much of Western culture promotes the individual hero, which creates excessive competition. Yes, we need to strive to be the best version of ourselves (self-leadership), but we can only achieve so much alone. To scale and multiply your impact, you need to grow people and build teams (people-leadership).

In sport, the concept of a team is well defined. Players have specific roles, such as forward, back, or goalkeeper, and the team has one objective, to score more points than the opposition in a specific time and win matches to achieve the championship. Each player is part of the team, and their individual efforts and their support of each other contribute to the team's results.

The sporting metaphor is used in business to describe teams, but the structure of a business team is more like an axle with spokes than a sports team. This is a workgroup and is distinct from a team. The key difference is that in a workgroup, you have a leader/manager forming an axle, with individuals of similar or different roles (reports) directly reporting to them, creating the spokes. There is little or no communication/collaboration between the reports or from the reports back to the leader.

Spokes can be functions or regions/geography. Unlike a team, the spokes do not collaborate, and the multiplying effect of a team is lost. Surprisingly this hub and spoke model is most prevalent in the organization's top team—the Executive Leadership Team.

CEOs typically think they have put together a team, but they have grouped competitors who must clamber for the CEO's attention, affirmation, and budget.

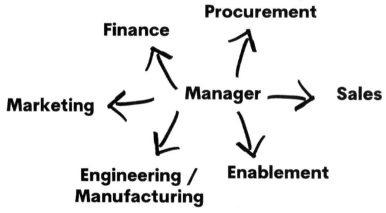

Figure 28: Workgroup 'spokes'

Hollywood has done a great job of depicting the sports coach/manager bringing together individual characters to forge a team, all wearing the same jersey and fighting for the same goal. We have witnessed the depiction of the inspirational locker-room speech where the coach implores players to put aside petty differences and play for the team.

Building a functional or executive leadership team is a bit different. The locker room is a company meeting, but these days is just as likely to be a Zoom call or a Google Hangout. However, the principles of building the team are the same:

1. Connect team members individual identity to the team identity.
2. Create psychological safety.
3. Communicate clear expectations—what success looks like, and the behaviors required to get there.
4. Foster belief—on the way to achieving objectives, the leader encourages the team to believe in themselves and the importance of the goal.
5. Hold accountability—through feedback and crucial conversations.
6. Promote bonding—a bonded team performs better, and the effective people manager knows that connection and bonding foundational human needs, especially when teams work remotely.
7. Celebrates the wins—sports teams dream of holding up the trophy, and corporate teams are no different. A good leader celebrates individual and team wins.

CHALLENGE:

1) ARE YOU LEADING A TEAM OR WORKGROUP?

2) WHAT CAN YOU DO TO CONNECT THE SPOKES?

Diversity Matters

A diverse mix of voices leads to better discussion, decisions, and outcomes for everyone.

—*Sundar Pichai, CEO of Google*

Ignoring diversity and inclusion will likely negatively impact you and your company's financial performance. According to McKinsey's 'Delivering through diversity' report (Jan 2018), gender, ethnic, and cultural diversity, particularly within executive teams, correlate to financial performance across multiple countries. What appears to drive this correlation is that more diverse companies can better attract top talent; improve their customer orientation, employee satisfaction, and decision-making; and secure their license to operate. So why is achieving diversity still a challenge?

You are smart, really smart. Your amazing brain can make judgments and decisions in milliseconds—unfortunately, you and the rest of us are often WRONG!

What's worse is we don't know we are wrong, and if it's pointed out to us, we are quick to justify our decisions.

Your ability to achieve lightning-fast decisions is by your brain taking shortcuts and using pattern recognition. For our ancestors to survive in a hostile environment, they needed to make quick judgments about friend or foe, food source or fatal, predator or pet. They made these judgments using what Daniel Kahneman, author of the book *Thinking Fast and Slow*, calls system one thinking. System one thinking is fast, instinctive, and emotional as opposed to system two thinking, which is slower, more deliberative, analytical, and logical.

Our brain has not had a firmware upgrade to help it operate in a modern, multicultural, and diverse workplace, so we regularly see the effects of system one thinking or unconscious bias when it comes to hiring, team building, recognition, and promotions. We can also fall prey to unconscious bias when making other types of decisions, such as investments.

By definition, unconscious bias is usually out of awareness, so how do we develop our awareness of what is often hidden?

In 2014, I received a call from the Women in Leadership program director at Singapore Management University, Dr Tanvi Gautam. She asked if I would teach a class on executive presence for her program.

Little did I know what a journey saying yes to that request would be.

I'm a son of a mother, a brother to two sisters, a husband to a wife, and a father to one daughter and one stepdaughter. My first profession was physiotherapy, which in the 80s when I studied and graduated, was dominated by women. Therefore, I considered myself inclusive and non-judgmental.

Executive presence, as we have discussed, is the ability to project gravitas, confidence, and poise under pressure, as well as reading the audience. This audience was going to be a test of my own executive presence.

Tanvi introduced me after lunch on day three of the program. I was the only male faculty, and this group of international women, mostly senior leaders, had already laughed, cried, and bonded. As I stepped into the center of the lecture auditorium, I had never felt so judged. Thirty pairs of eyes stared at me as if I was the enemy; not a single smile was present.

It was as if I was the personification of every man that had discounted, discouraged, or undermined these women. If this had been my first speaking engagement, I would have cut and run, vowing never to do it again. But it wasn't. I abandoned my lesson plan and asked the group to partner with someone next to them to share the adjectives that entered their heads when they first saw me. After doing this, I asked them to share either their adjectives or their partner's, thus giving some plausible deniability.

They did not hold back. Arrogant, aggressive, alpha male were typical responses. I also received professional, knowledgable, and courageous.

So far, I had said and done nothing other than to ask them the adjective question and to share their responses. These adjectives, which indicated judgments, were pure projections on the part of the students. I pointed this out and invited the group to get to know me as a person rather than by my gender. I shared that I was a father and had looked after my children after their mother left me. I shared the work I do for at-risk and disadvantaged teenagers and the work I was doing to elevate women leaders.

'Has any of this changed your initial perception?' I asked. For many of the students, it had, whilst others held steadfastly to their first-impression bias. Yes, I'm male, white, bald, and quite well built, and perhaps I could pass for an aging nightclub bouncer, but my gender and physical attributes don't represent who I am. I then illustrated that I now knew how they must feel when they are judged on their gender, age, or ethnicity. The irony was that this group of women leaders had fallen into the same trap of judging a book by its cover.

The more you know people for 'who' they are, the less you judge them for 'what' they are.

—Dr Tanvi Gautam

I share this story because diversity means overcoming our natural bias to judge people unfairly when they don't look like us.

I was working with a former CEO of DSO National Laboratories to help get his senior leaders to be more open to input from different perspectives, including from younger employees.

'Nobody has a monopoly on good ideas,' he said.

Wow! I thought. What a great mantra for diversity, inclusion, leadership, management, and just common sense. But as Winston Churchill once remarked, 'Nothing is as uncommon as common sense.'

For survival, the human mind is hard-wired to consider ideas and perspectives from our own tribe as safer and, therefore, superior to information from outsiders. This human tendency leads to political partisanship and to leadership teams that look and think the same. The dangers of this 'we are right, everybody else is wrong' mindset are obvious, especially in times of rapid change when past ways of doing things have lost their relevancy.

If a closed mindset and in-the-box thinking is the default setting, what must leaders do to override this and upgrade to inclusive leadership and diversity of thought?

Before I explain how, let's look at why.

Research by Deloitte makes a compelling case for diversity and inclusive leadership. Teams with inclusive leaders are:

- 17% more likely to report being a high performing team
- 20% more likely to say they make high-quality decisions
- 29% more likely to report behaving collaboratively.

My diversity of thought and inclusive leadership gets tested every time I step in front of a group to facilitate or coach. It's not uncommon for me to have leaders from eight to ten different countries and cultures, some who won't speak up and some who can't keep quiet. Navigating a minefield of sensitivities whilst challenging perspectives is what gets my blood racing.

Surprisingly, many leaders who practice the behaviors of diversity and inclusive leadership are unaware that this is what they are doing, and those who don't practice these behaviors are under the impression that they are inclusive. The reason is simple: mindset. Diversity and inclusion are a mindset that sees people of different genders and 'tribes' as all people; their differences don't register, just their contribution.

The mindset of the non-diverse or inclusive leaders means they see nothing wrong in the following behaviors:

- being overpowering—not letting others speak, not inviting other inputs or perspectives
- discounting—putting down, ridiculing, or ignoring any idea not generated by themselves or their 'tribe'
- obvious bias—only a select group of people are ever given opportunities to give opinions or make decisions.

So, if these narrow-minded and divisive behaviors are toxic to the growth and sustainability of a company, what mindsets and behaviors should be encouraged?

The most powerful mindset a leader could adopt is humility. I don't mean humility in the sense of making yourself less than you are but in the true meaning of humility, which is grounded. The grounded leader knows what they are good at and their weaknesses. The grounded leader is aware that their perspective is just a perspective and can consider alternative, even contradictory, views as equally valid.

With this truly humble mindset, the inclusive leader will:

- create a psychologically safe space for discussion
- admit their weaknesses as well as their strengths
- ask for feedback on their blind spots
- actively seek out differing perspectives
- be informed of cultural differences
- treat people as individuals with something to offer
- ensure they are making decisions on the best ideas, irrespective of where they come from.

Turn on the news today, and you will see graphic images and hear stories of racism, discrimination, and prejudice. We witness politicians stoking fear for political gain and see the disenfranchised exercising their frustration at injustice. Meanwhile, in corporate boardrooms and executive team meetings, there is talk of the need for diversity and inclusion, and sometimes there is action. Unfortunately, it's hard to make the changes when you are inside the box of your own unconscious bias.

If you want inspiration that a shift of perspective is possible, I recommend the movie *Hidden Figures* (Melfi, 2016), which is based on a book of the same name (Shetterly, 2016). The story is about female African American mathematicians who worked at NASA during the Space Race.

Diversity isn't easy, but neither is going to the moon—and we only accomplished that through diversity.

One leader, that I got to know in Singapore, through being his coach is, Nadim Mohr. Nadim is currently the Head of APAC, Environment Science at Bayer. Nadim builds very effective diverse teams because his own unique experiences allow him to overcome bias and look only for competence.

Nadim was born in New York, of Dutch parents. His Grandfather was born in the Netherlands although his six older siblings were born in Indonesia. In fact, the family wasn't Dutch at all, they were German, but became Dutch so that they could legally buy property in Indonesia.

Nadim went to school in New York until he was nine, then in Paris, then in Geneva, but finished high school in Côte d'Ivoire. He did is undergraduate degree in Rome and his master's degree in London. After graduating he went back to the Ivory Coast for his first real job, but although he had lived in Africa during school he experienced a lot of racism, being the only Caucasian in an African company. He returned to New York to work, but the apartment he was living in collapsed because of the Twin Towers attack on 9/11. He thought about going back to Africa, but his father said, try something new and go to Asia.

Nadim bought a ticket to Bangkok, with the intention of traveling around. After a week, he bumped into someone who he knew from New York, who was managing his company making mosquito nets. He was offered an internship at this company but after two months, they offered to make him marketing manager, and after six months, they asked him to become the managing director.

Nadim often tells his team that, "diversity sucks"; everyone, including himself, would at times prefer to be surrounded by likeminded people. His own unique story has meant that the number of similar people is scarce and so he has experienced the power that diversity brings, and his position enables him to give back for the opportunities he was given.

This has led Nadim to constantly check his own biases, to get out of his own way and ensure that diversity is at the heart of every team he develops.

Nadim has learned, as we all must, to see the person, not a label, and be curious about what that person can bring, and not be afraid of the difference.

If we want to be human whilst delivering accelerated results we must, for now, use positive bias to counter long held negative biases. We will reap the results through commitment to building truly diverse teams, because nobody has a monopoly on good ideas!

CHALLENGE:

HOW DIVERSE IS YOUR TEAM? WHAT ARE YOU DOING TO OVERCOME BIAS AND ACTIVELY SEEK DIVERSE PERSPECTIVES?

PART 5: THE FUTURE OF WORK

The intention of this book has been to provide you with principles and plays to be human whilst delivering accelerated results. Occasionally I have referenced the context and environment you will be doing that in, but it would be remiss of me not to provide some ideas and insights on navigating the new reality we all find ourselves in. COVID-19 has changed the work landscape; perhaps it just accelerated a transformation that was imminent, but the change was sudden and tangible, and there is no going back.

Talking to leaders of traditional organizations, going back to work is exactly what they think will happen as we put the pandemic behind us, but this ignores the seismic shift that has happened with employer-employee relations. Employees want the freedom to work from home, and *the great resignation* cannot be ignored. The great resignation refers to the massive spike in resignations as job openings remain elevated. This is a global phenomenon as people face digital burnout amid COVID-19 due to a sense of isolation and loss of networks.

Resignation has an economic, human, and productivity cost. I spoke with an experienced human resource (HR) leader and former head of talent at Deloitte, Herdis Pala Palsdottir. Herdis noted that in her experience, many executives tended to overlook the cost of employee resignation and rehiring. One reason is that it may not be costing them a lot directly if they are not using external agencies to hire. However, the indirect cost can be very high as you will be eating up most of HR´s time.

Managers might notice the cost in terms of productivity as manpower and experience leaves, but what about the human cost? People join a company with hopes and dreams as well as for the paycheck. Resignation leaves a bad taste for the leaver and can destroy the morale of those who stay, as they wonder if they should leave too. The survivors will be the first to greet your new hires and the ones interfacing with your customers, who will be asking why their contact has left the company.

Many studies show that the total cost of losing an employee can range from tens of thousands of dollars to two times their annual salary, so leadership needs to be invested in this matter and analyze what can be done.

I have covered several strategies in this book that positively impact employee engagement and retention, thus making human and economic sense. These include:

- what makes a good manager
- setting clear expectations
- mindset and motivation
- communicating with *why*
- giving effective feedback
- encouraging ownership and self-leadership
- building confidence
- reducing conflict and increasing collaboration
- having career conversations

- creating a culture where people feel safe
- coaching for development
- encouraging diversity.

Whilst these strategies may not be enough to fully inoculate against the great resignation, they will help as things stabilize. The pandemic caused workers to rethink their careers, work conditions, and long-term goals. According to a study conducted by Adobe, Millennials and Generation Z are driving the exodus, as they are more likely to be dissatisfied with their jobs. More than half of Gen Z reported planning to seek a new job within the next year. But what will that job look like?

Catalyzed by the pandemic, smart companies have already embraced the concept of a distributed workforce. Microsoft, for example, announced that working from home is a permanent solution for most of its employees. So is the office dead?

Ninety percent of employees surveyed said they never want to return to the office full-time. At the same time, people are missing the community aspect of work, and some are experiencing increasing stress from juggling home and work duties. The solution is to rethink the office. Here are seven things to ponder:

1. The office headquarters may be dead, but offices will persist. They will be used less frequently, then hardly at all. More co-working spaces will be created to allow workers who prefer that mode of work to operate from there.

2. Remote retreats—purpose-built destinations that allow entire companies to fly in for a synchronous week—will likely become commonplace. These retreats could be staffed with facilitators and educators who train employees to maximize effectiveness and communication.

3. Companies will hire the best talent, not based on geography, gender, age, or any other bias. This will lead to the most diverse and inclusive teams and create a competitive advantage for those companies who move quickly on this mindset.

4. Fewer pointless meetings. Wasting hours traveling to a meeting is over. Instead, conferences and quarterly networking events will become more intentional for cultivating in-person relationships and collective brainstorming.

5. Companies will need to embrace tools for asynchronous work. This might include robotic processes to pass work from one employee to another. It will also mean workers can do what they are good at, and menial or repetitive tasks can be outsourced or automated.

6. Communication must evolve. With less or no face-to-face time, leaders and employees must become more efficient in communicating concrete expectations of performance and abstract ideas like values and culture.

7. Rather than worry whether employees are working whilst at home, companies will need to be concerned that they are not overworking. With extra time gained from the lack of commute, employees should be encouraged to take time out for healthy and social activities. The stigma of not being at your desk needs to be replaced by the sense of satisfaction of delivering quality output in an enjoyable and sustainable way.

REFLECTION:

AFTER READING THIS LIST, HOW ADAPTABLE ARE YOU TO THE NEW WAY OF WORKING? WHAT MINDSET AND BEHAVIORS DO YOU NEED TO FOCUS ON TO BE HUMAN WHILST DELIVERING ACCELERATED RESULTS?

In the past, companies would rely on pay and benefits to motivate and retain people, but income is not a measure of wealth, just as health is not a measure of wellness. Health is the absence of disease, whereas wellness is as an abundance of energy and purpose. Likewise, income might be the absence of poverty but not the abundance of choices.

Counterintuitive as it might be, research (Lyubomirsky, 2007) clearly shows that money beyond a certain threshold does not make us any happier. Let me illustrate: Imagine you are lost in the woods, cold, wet, and hungry. You stumble across a cottage with an open door; there is the glow of a warm fire and the smell of stew and fresh bread. A friendly person welcomes you in, wraps you in a blanket, sits you by the fire, and feeds you. Your happiness would increase significantly from the thirty minutes before, and receiving a large amount of money wouldn't even register on the happiness scale.

So, if money beyond a certain threshold doesn't make a difference—what does? Choices do, well, more specifically, the right choices.

This book provides you with a framework and plays, which, if you choose to apply, will make you a better manager or leader. But why?

Here are seven questions I regularly ask myself and share with my coaching clients:

1. What kind of work gives you the most satisfaction?
2. What kind of work that you can do gives the most contribution?
3. What are you doing for self-care?
4. What are you doing to grow as a person?
5. What will be your legacy at work and for your family and community?
6. What level of influence do you want to have?
7. What is your plan to integrate the previous six points?

I'm not prescribing this list; I'm just sharing it as a thought provoker. I don't have a problem with high goals and making lots of money, but I do caution about having narrow goals and losing your humanity.

The pandemic flushed out some of the worst kinds of selfishness and stupidity, and in fear, people forgot the benefits of community and contribution. In my story about getting lost in the woods, who was happier—you or the person providing shelter?

When you understand this question and the answer, you will appreciate the perspective I'm sharing here.

> **REFLECTION:**
> **HOW CAN YOU BE THE BEST VERSION OF YOURSELF AND CREATE A LEGACY TODAY?**

FINAL THOUGHTS

On 16 December 2019 (with about 4,000 other people in Singapore), I had the pleasure of listening to insights and perspectives from Barack Obama, the forty-fourth President of the United States.

Regardless of your nationality or politics, Obama held the most visible leadership position on the planet, and for that he deserves some respect. Personally, I enjoyed his humorous oratory style and watching him riff on a wide range of topics with an intoxicating mix of humility and gravitas.

Here are some takeaways on leadership from listening to Obama in 2019:

1) Anyone in a leadership position needs to build an effective team of people who are smart and have integrity—then get out of their way.

2) A lot of the problems in the world are caused by old men who stayed too long and confused their personal interests with that of the nation.

3) We need more women in national leadership—imagine if every country in the world was run by women for just two years.

4) We need leaders who understand complexity and don't just go for the quick, easy answer. This requires followers who are also interested and tolerant of that complexity.

5) When it comes to making a complex decision, ask yourself, 'Does this make things better?' If the answer is yes, make the decision.

6) Realize that as a leader, you are in a relay race. You take the baton, run with it, and then pass it on to the next person.

7) All our problems won't be solved in our lifetime, but we live in the most amazing period in human history, so enjoy it and look to the next generation.

Whilst this list is clearly about political leadership, it is optimistic, and I hope you will agree that we have addressed many of his points in this book. We have explored building the team, the benefits of diversity, the importance of decisiveness, and we have touched on legacy.

As I finish this final chapter, it's the end of a busy day working from my home in Portugal. I started my day online coaching a C-level executive in Singapore. I then confirmed with my speaker bureau in Sweden for an in-person speech in Stockholm. I have had virtual meetings with my team members in the Philippines, Ukraine, and the United Kingdom. I'm about to jump on a call with a coach in Houston, Texas, and I will send this manuscript to my editor and publisher in Australia. I usually squeeze in a long walk for health and mindfulness, but today it is a bit cold, so I played online chess with my son. Is this the future of work?

With the freelancers that work for me, I ensure they understand my principles and why it's important to share the insights and information I have through books, speeches, coaching, and online programs. I give them regular feedback on what they are doing well and how they can improve and celebrate when we hit milestones. Just like I did when I had a physical office with permanent staff.

So, my final thought is that you might not get to be the leader of your country, but if you lead even one person, you are positively impacting them, and that positively impacts the people around them.

To your success, Andrew Bryant

REFERENCES

Bass, B. M. (1981), *Stodgill's Handbook of Leadership: A Survey of Theory and Research*, New York: Free Press.

Bass, B. M. (1985), *Leadership and Performance Beyond Expectation*, Free Press.

Blanchard, K. & Johnson, S. (1994), *The One Minute Manager*, Harper Collins.

Bohn, H. G. (1885), *Hand-book of Proverbs*.

Bossidy, C. B. (2002), *Execution: The Discipline of Getting Things Done*, Currency.

Bryant, A. (2016), *Self Leadership - 12 Powerful Mindsets & Methods to Win in Life & Business*, Self Published (Amazon).

Bryant, A. & Kazan, A. (2012), *Self Leadership: How to Become a More Successful, Effective and Efficient Leader from the Inside Out*, McGraw Hill.

Burns, J. M. (1978), *Leadership*, Harper and Row.

CFI Education Inc. (2022), *Ansoff Matrix*, Corporate Finance Institute, https://corporatefinanceinstitute.com/resources/knowledge/strategy/ansoff-matrix/

Collins, J. (2001), *Good to Great*, Harper Collins.

Deloitte (2014), *The Collaborative Economy*.

Dondi, M., Klier, J., Panier, F., & Schubert, J. (2021, June 25), *Defining the skills citizens will need in the future world of work*, McKinsey and

Company, Retrieved November, 2021, from https://www.mckinsey. com/industries/public-and-social-sector/our-insights/defining-the-skills-citizens-will-need-in-the-future-world-of-work

Drucker, P. (1954), *The Practice of Management*, Harper, New York.

Dweck, C. S. (2007), *Mindset: The New Psychology of Success*, Ballantine Books.

Economy, P. (n.d), *Inc.com*, https://www.linkedin.com/posts/andrewbryant_ facebook-instagram-selfawareness-activity-6851051944140779520-6HEi.

Frankl, V. E. (1946), *Man's Search for Meaning*, Beacon Press.

Galway, T. W. (1997), *The Inner Game of Tennis: The Classic Guide to the Mental Side of Peak Performance*, Random House.

Henley, W. (1888), *Book of Verses*.

House, R. J. (1971), A Path Goal Theory of Leader Effectiveness, *Administrative Science Quarterly, 16* (3), 321–339.

House, R. J. & Mitchell, T. R. (1974), Path–Goal Theory of Leadership, *Journal of Contemporary Business, 3* (4), 1-97.

Kawasaki, G. (2019), *https://www.cnbc.com/2019/03/01/former-apple-employee-guy-kawasaki-once-stood-up-to-steve-jobs-here-is-the-amazing-response-he-received.html*

Kruger, D. & Dunning, D. (1999), Unaware of It: How Difficulties in Recognizing One's Own Incompetence Lead to Inflated Self-Assessments' *Journal of Personality and Social Psychology*

Leadership principles. Amazon jobs, Retrieved November, 2021, from https://www.amazon.jobs/en/principles

Lencioni, P. (2002), *The Five Dysfunctions of a Team*, Jossey-Bass.

Lonczak, H. S. (2021), *PositivePsychology.com*, https://positivepsychology. com/positive-reinforcement-workplace/.

McKinsey. (2021), 'Defining the skills citizens will need in the future world of work.'

Patterson, K. & Grenny, J. (2011), *Crucial Conversations: Tools for Talking When Stakes Are High*, McGraw Hill.

Platow, M. J., Haslam, A. S., & Reicher, S. D. (2019), *The Oxford Handbook of Social Influence*, Oxford University Press.

References

Rosenberg, M. B. (2003), *Nonviolent Communication*, Puddle Dancer Press.

Shetterly, M. (2016), *Hidden Figures*, William Morrow and Company.

Sinek, S. (2011), *Start with Why*, Penguin Books Ltd.

Trompenaars, F. & Hamden-Turner, C. (1996), *Riding the Waves of Culture: Understanding Diversity in Global Business*, Nicholas Brealey Publishing Ltd.

Tuckman, B. W. (1965), Developmental Sequence in Small Groups, *Psychological Bulletin*

Vroom, V. H. (1964), *Work and Motivation*, Wiley.

World Health Organization (n.d.), *WHO remains firmly committed to the principles set out in the preamble to the Constitution*, https://www.who.int/about/governance/constitution.